COMPUTER SCIENCE, TECHNOLOGY AND APPLICATIONS

IMAGE FUSION

PRINCIPLES, TECHNOLOGY AND APPLICATIONS

COMPUTER SCIENCE, TECHNOLOGY AND APPLICATIONS

Additional books in this series can be found on Nova's website under the Series tab.

Additional E-books in this series can be found on Nova's website under the E-book tab.

COMPUTER SCIENCE, TECHNOLOGY AND APPLICATIONS

IMAGE FUSION

PRINCIPLES, TECHNOLOGY AND APPLICATIONS

CHRISTOPHER T. DAVIS
EDITOR

nova publishers
New York

Library of Congress Cataloging-in-Publication Data

Image fusion : principles, technology, and applications / editors, Christopher T. Davis.
pages cm. -- (Computer science, technology, and applications)
Includes bibliographical references and index.
ISBN 978-1-63482-115-5 (hardcover)
1. Multispectral imaging. 2. Computer vision. I. Davis, Christopher T., editor.
TA1634.I48 2015
006.3'7--dc23

2015002247

Published by Nova Science Publishers, Inc. † New York

CONTENTS

Preface		**vii**
Chapter 1	Performance Assessment in Image Fusion *Gemma Piella*	**1**
Chapter 2	Saliency Based Framework for Thermal and Visual Image Fusion *Ashirbani Saha, Gaurav Bhatnagar and Q. M. Jonathan Wu*	**17**
Chapter 3	Fusion of Multifocus Color Images from Microscopic Samples Using the Modulus of the Gradient of the Color Planes *Carina Toxqui-Quitl, Román Hurtado-Pérez, Alfonso Padilla-Vivanco and Gabriel Ortega-Mendoza*	**45**
Chapter 4	Fusion and Classification of Multisource Images for Update of Forest GIS *D. Amarsaikhan and N. Ganchuluun*	**83**
Chapter 5	Multimodal Medical Image Fusion Based on SUSAN Feature in Framelet Domain *Gaurav Bhatnagar*	**121**
Index		**153**

PREFACE

The widespread use of image fusion methods (e.g., in military applications, surveillance or medical diagnostics), has increased the need for pertinent performance or quality assessment tools to compare results obtained with different algorithms or to obtain an optimal setting of parameters for a given fusion algorithm. This book discusses principles, different technologies and applications of image fusion.

Chapter 1 presents different measures to evaluate image fusion based on the structural similarity between the inputs and the fused image. These measures do not require a ground-truth and are easy to compute. They are compliant with subjective evaluations and can therefore be used to compare different image fusion methods or to find the best parameters for a given fusion algorithm.

In Chapter 2, the authors propose an efficient framework for integrating or fusing thermal and visual images. This category of fusion finds application in navigation and surveillance systems. The main idea in this category of fusion is to successfully extract significant information from both of the thermal and visual images and combine them to form the fused image. The fused image has better representation of the entire scene as compared to the source images alone. Since, human beings are the principal judge of navigation and surveillance systems, the authors explore the ability of visual attention property of the human visual system (HVS) to generate the fused image. Generally, techniques for modeling the visual attention generate saliency maps in order to highlight the relative importance of pixels (or regions) in any image based on HVS. In the proposed approach, the authors use saliency maps from the source images to combine the significant thermal information with the significant visual information. The saliency maps serve two purposes. Firstly, they highlight the salient areas in the thermal and visual images. Secondly, the saliency values are also used to compute weights to generate the final fused image. Hence, the salient parts of the visual and thermal images are retained in the fused image. Different types of visual attention modeling techniques are used in the framework to demonstrate their relative performance in thermal and visual image fusion. Though the chosen modeling technique plays a key role in the performance of the fusion framework, the authors' experiments on various image sets demonstrate the promise of the proposed approach in terms of visual inspection and different objective evaluation criteria. The novelty of the approach lies in developing a framework for saliency based fusion of thermal and visual information.

Commonly in the light microscopy, the limited Depth-of-Field (DOF) of an imaging system causes blur images when the sample is wider than the DOF of the optical system. Additionally, the DOF decreases as the magnification increases. In order to extend the DOF of a microscopic system Chapter 3 proposes a multi-focus image fusion method based on the modulus of the gradient color planes. This procedure is applied to multi-focus microscopy color images which have been acquired by the bright-field reflection microscopy technique. Our results are obtained using real specimens and any post-processing step is done over the fused image. The proposed method is simple, fast and practically free of artifacts or false color.

The main objectives of Chapter 4 are to evaluate the performances of different image fusion techniques for the enhancement of spectral and textural variations of different forest types and to apply are fined maximum likelihood classifier for the extraction of forest class information from the fused images in order to update a forest geographical information system (GIS). For the data fusion, modified intensity-hue-saturation (IHS) transformation, principal components analysis (PCA) method, Gram-Schmidt fusion, color normalization spectral sharpening, wavelet-based method, and Ehlers fusion are used and the results are compared. Of these methods, the better results are obtained through the use of the modified IHS transformation, PCA and wavelet-based fusion. The refined classification method uses spatial thresholds defined from contextual knowledge and different features obtained through a feature derivation process. The result of the refined classification is compared with the results of a standard method and it demonstrates a higher accuracy. Overall, the research indicates that multisource data fusion can significantly improve the interpretation and classification of forest types and the elaborated refined classification method is a powerful tool to increase classification accuracy.

Multimodal medical image fusion is an important task for the retrieval of complementary information from medical images. In Chapter 5, a novel framework for multimodal medical image fusion is proposed, which enables the decomposition of input images into low- and high frequency bands using framelet transform and utilizes local visibility and smallest univalue segment assimilating nucleus (SUSAN) features fusion rules for coefficient selection at different levels. The final fused image is obtained from the superposition of selected coefficients in bot low- and high- frequency bands. The fused medical image that is produced by this framework presents a visually better representation than the input images. Experimental results highlights the expediency and suitability of the proposed algorithm and the efficiency is carried by the comparison made between proposed and existing algorithm.

In: Image Fusion
Editor: C. T. Davis, pp. 1-15
ISBN: 978-1-63482-115-5

Chapter 1

PERFORMANCE ASSESSMENT IN IMAGE FUSION

Gemma Piella*
DTIC, Universitat Pompeu Fabra, Barcelona, Spain

Abstract

We present different measures to evaluate image fusion based on the structural similarity between the inputs and the fused image. These measures do not require a ground-truth and are easy to compute. They are compliant with subjective evaluations and can therefore be used to compare different image fusion methods or to find the best parameters for a given fusion algorithm.

Keywords: image fusion, image quality, assessment
AMS Subject Classification: 68U10

1. Introduction

The widespread use of image fusion methods (e.g. in military applications, surveillance or medical diagnostics), has increased the need for pertinent performance or quality assessment tools to compare results obtained with different algorithms or to obtain an optimal setting of parameters for a given fusion algorithm.

*E-mail address: gemma.piella@upf.edu

In most cases, image fusion is only a preparatory step to some specific task such as human monitoring, and thus the performance of the fusion algorithm has to be measured in terms of improvement of the subsequent tasks. For example, in classification tasks, a common evaluation measure is the percentage of correct classifications. This requires that the 'true' correct classifications are known. In experimental setups, however, the availability of a ground-truth is not guaranteed.

In this chapter, we focus on image fusion performance measures which can be computed independently of the subsequent task. More precisely, we are interested in measures that express the successfulness of an image fusion technique by the extent that it creates a fused image that retains salient information from the sources while minimizing the number of artifacts or the amount of distortion that could interfere with interpretation.

In Section 2, we briefly review the state-of-the art methods for measuring fusion performance. In Section 3, we present some variants of a quality measure for image fusion. The interest of these measures, which are based on the structural similarity index introduced by Wang et al. in [20, 21], lies in the fact that they do not require a ground-truth or reference image and are easy to compute. In Section 4, we use these measures to evaluate fused images. Results show that such measures are compliant with subjective evaluations and can therefore be used to compare different image fusion methods or to find the best parameters for a specific fusion algorithm.

2. Existing Approaches to Image Fusion Performance

In many applications, the end user or interpreter of the fusion result is a human. Thus, human perception of the fused image is of paramount importance and therefore, fusion results are often evaluated by subjective criteria [13, 16, 9]. This involves human observers to judge the *quality* of the resulting images. As such a 'human quality measure' depends highly on psychovisual factors, these subjective tests are difficult to reproduce or verify. Furthermore, they are time consuming and expensive. This shows clearly the need for objective measures that quantify the performance of fusion algorithms. The key problem is how to quantify a subjective impression like image quality. One way to 'solve' this problem is by associating quality with the deviation of the experimental fused image from the 'ideal' one [18, 5, 19]. Then, another problem arises, namely, how to define the 'ideal' fused image. An alternative approach is to quantify the quality based solely in the fused image; that is, without reference to the source images or a ground-truth. In this case, any objective non-reference quality image can be used. For example, contrast-to-noise ratio, entropy or gradient strength have been used [8, 6]. Finally, another approach is to design performance measures which, without assuming knowledge of a ground-truth, can be used for quality assessment of the fused image by quantifying the degree to which the fused image is 'related' to the input sources [24, 12, 11, 4].

Examples of reference-based quality measures for fusion

Various fusion algorithms presented in the literature have been evaluated by constructing some kind of ideal fused image x_R and comparing with the experimental fused result x_F [7, 18, 5, 19]. In this case, fusion evaluation amounts to measure the distortion or dissimilarity between x_R and x_F. The smaller the distortion, the better the quality of the fused image.

The l^2-metric (i.e., root mean squared error), given by

$$d_2(x_R, x_F) = \left(\frac{1}{MN} \sum_{m=1}^{M} \sum_{n=1}^{N} \big(x_R(m,n) - x_F(m,n)\big)^2 \right)^{1/2} \tag{1}$$

(where M, N are the dimensions of the images), is widely used for such purposes, notwithstanding its well-known limitations. In a certain way, it measures the total amount of energy distortion. High errors correspond to high distortions. Directly related measures are the signal to noise ratio and the peak signal to noise ratio.

Another class of measures is based on concepts from information theory. The empirical *mutual information* is often used for fusion evaluation:

$$I(x_R; x_F) = \sum_{u=1}^{L} \sum_{v=1}^{L} p_{R,F}(u,v) \log_2 \frac{p_{R,F}(u,v)}{p_R(u) p_F(v)}, \tag{2}$$

where p_R, p_F are the normalized graylevel histograms of x_R, x_F, respectively, $p_{R,F}$ is the joint graylevel histogram of x_R and x_F, and L is the number of bins. The measure $I(x_R; x_F)$ indicates how much information the fused image x_F conveys about the reference x_R. Thus, the higher the mutual information between x_F and x_R, the more x_F resembles the ideal x_R. In this sense, mutual information can be interpreted as a 'similarity' measure, in contrast with the l^2-metric in (1) which can be seen as a 'dissimilarity' (i.e., distortion) measure. Ideally, one has $I(x_R; x_F) = H(x_R)$, where H is the empirical entropy, although this does not imply that $x_R = x_F$.

Examples of non-reference quality measures for fusion
An example of an objective performance measure which does not assume the knowledge of a ground-truth was given by Xydeas and Petrović in [24]. Their performance measure models the accuracy with which visual information is transferred from the source images to the fused image. In their approach, important visual information is associated with edge information measured for each pixel. Thus, they measure the fusion performance by evaluating the relative amount of edge information that is transferred from the input images to the fused image. This amount is normalized to the range $[0, 1]$, so that value 0 corresponds to the 'complete loss' of edge information from the sources to the output x_F, and value 1 to the 'total preservation'.

Another non-reference objective performance measure was proposed by Qu et al. in [12]. They evaluate fusion performance by adding the mutual information between the fused image and each of the input images, i.e., they compute

$$I(x_A; x_F) + I(x_B; x_F)\,, \tag{3}$$

where x_A, x_B are the input images to be fused and I is computed as in (2). The higher the value in (3), the better the quality of the fused image is supposed to be.

Other examples of non-reference objective performance measure are those based on the structural similarity index, presented on the next section, and those proposed in [1, 2, 14, 4, 10].

3. A Structural Quality Measure for Image Fusion

This section discusses an objective non-reference quality assessment method for image fusion that utilizes local measurements to estimate how well salient information contained within the sources is represented by the fused image. The method, based on the structural similarity index [20, 21], was first proposed in [11]. Variants include [3, 25, 26].

3.1. The Structural Similarity Index

We present a brief introduction to the structural image similarity index that was introduced by Wang et al. in [20, 21]. Given two images x and y of size $M \times N$, let $\bar{x}$ denote the mean of x and σ_x^2, σ_{xy} the variance of x and covariance of x, y, respectively, i.e.,

$$\begin{aligned}\sigma_x^2 &= \frac{1}{MN-1}\sum_{m=1}^{M}\sum_{n=1}^{N}\left(x(m,n)-\bar{x}\right)^2\\ \sigma_{xy} &= \frac{1}{MN-1}\sum_{m=1}^{M}\sum_{n=1}^{N}\left(x(m,n)-\bar{x}\right)\left(y(m,n)-\bar{y}\right).\end{aligned}$$

The structural similarity index (SSIM) is defined by

$$Q_0(x,y)=\frac{(2\bar{x}\bar{y}+C_1)(2\sigma_{xy}+C_2)}{(\bar{x}^2+\bar{y}^2+C_1)(\sigma_x^2+\sigma_y^2+C_2)},$$

which can be decomposed as

$$Q_0(x,y)=\frac{2\bar{x}\bar{y}+C_1}{\bar{x}^2+\bar{y}^2+C_1}\cdot\frac{2\sigma_x\sigma_y+C_2}{\sigma_x^2+\sigma_y^2+C_2}\cdot\frac{\sigma_{xy}+C_2/2}{\sigma_x\sigma_y+C_2/2}, \tag{4}$$

where C_1, C_2 are small constants to avoid the denominator to be zero. This index measures the similarity of images x and y, and takes values between -1 and 1. The first component in (4) corresponds to a kind of average luminance distortion and it has a dynamic range of $[0,1]$ (assuming nonnegative mean values). The second component measures a contrast distortion and its range is also $[0,1]$. The third factor is the correlation coefficient between x and y. The maximum value $Q_0 = 1$ is achieved when x and y are identical.

Since image signals are generally non-stationary, it is appropriate to measure the number Q_0 over local regions and then combine the different results into a single measure. Wang et al. [20, 21] proposed to use a sliding window approach: starting from the top-left corner of the two images x, y, a sliding window of fixed size moves pixel by pixel over the entire image until the bottom-right corner is reached. For each window w, the local quality index $Q_0(x, y \mid w)$ is computed for the values $x(m,n)$ and $y(m,n)$ where pixels (m,n) lie in the sliding window w. Finally, the overall image quality index Q_0 is computed by averaging all local quality indices:

$$Q_0(x,y)=\frac{1}{|W|}\sum_{w\in W}Q_0(x,y\mid w), \tag{5}$$

where W is the family of all windows and $|W|$ is the cardinality of W.

The structural similarity index and its variants have been compared (under several types of distortions) to existing image measures such as the mean squared error (MSE) or visual information fidelity (VIF) [15]. The main conclusion is that it exhibits similar performance to VIF, outperforming the MSE in terms of correlation with subjective evaluations. This is due to the index's ability of measuring structural distortions, in contrast to the MSE which is highly sensitive to the l^2-energy of errors.

3.2. A SSIM-based Fusion Quality Measure

We use the image quality index Q_0 defined in (5) to define a quality measure $Q(x_A, x_B, x_F)$ for image fusion which should express the 'quality' of x_F given the inputs x_A, x_B.

We denote by $s(x_A|w)$ the saliency of image x_A in window w. It should reflect the local relevance of image x_A within the window w, and it may depend on, e.g., contrast, variance, or entropy. Given the local saliencies $s(x_A|w)$ and $s(x_B|w)$ of the two input images, we compute a local weight $\lambda(w)$ between 0 and 1 indicating the relative importance of image x_A compared to image x_B: the larger $\lambda(w)$, the more weight is given to image x_A. A simple choice for $\lambda(w)$ is

$$\lambda(w) = \frac{s(x_A|w)}{s(x_A|w) + s(x_B|w)} . \tag{6}$$

We define the fusion quality measure $Q(x_A, x_B, x_F)$ as

$$Q(x_A, x_B, x_F) = \frac{1}{|W|} \sum_{w \in W} \Big(\lambda(w) Q_0(x_A, x_F|w) + (1 - \lambda(w)) Q_0(x_B, x_F|w) \Big) . \tag{7}$$

Thus, in regions where image x_A has a large saliency compared to x_B, the quality measure $Q(x_A, x_B, x_F)$ is mainly determined by the 'similarity' of x_F and input image x_A. On the other hand, in regions where the saliency of x_B is much larger than that of x_A, the measure $Q(x_A, x_B, x_F)$ is determined mostly by the 'similarity' of x_F and input image x_B.

At this point, our model has produced a quality measure which gives an indication of how much of the salient information contained in each of the input images has been transferred into the fused image. However, the different quality measures obtained within each window have been treated equally. This is in contrast with the human visual system which is known to give higher importance to visually salient regions in an image. We now define another variant of the fusion quality measure by giving more weight to those windows where the saliency of the input images is higher. These correspond to areas which are likely to be perceptually important parts of the underlying scene. Therefore, the quality of the fused image in those areas is of more importance when determining the overall quality. The saliency of a window can be defined as $C(w) = \max\{s(x_A|w), s(x_B|w)\}$. The *weighted fusion quality measure* is then obtained as

$$Q_W(x_A, x_B, x_F) = \sum_{w \in W} c(w)\Big(\lambda(w)Q_0(x_A, x_F|w) + \big(1 - \lambda(w)\big)Q_0(x_B, x_F|w)\Big), \tag{8}$$

where $c(w) = C(w)/\big(\sum_{w' \in W} C(w')\big)$. There are various other ways to compute the weights $c(w)$ (for example, we could define $C(w) = s(x_A|w) + s(x_B|w)$), but we have found that the choice made here is a good indicator of important areas in the input images.

We introduce one final modification of the fusion quality measure that takes into account some aspect of the human visual system, namely the importance of edge information. Note that we can evaluate Q_W in (8) using 'edge images' (e.g., the norm of the gradient) instead of the original grayscale images x_A, x_B and x_F. Let us denote the edge image corresponding with x_A by x'_A. Now we combine $Q_W(x_A, x_B, x_F)$ and $Q_W(x'_A, x'_B, x'_F)$ into a so-called *edge-dependent fusion quality measure* by

$$Q_E(x_A, x_B, x_F) = Q_W(x_A, x_B, x_F)^{1-\alpha} \cdot Q_W(x'_A, x'_B, x'_F)^{\alpha}\,, \tag{9}$$

where the parameter $\alpha \in [0, 1]$ expresses the contribution of the edge image compared to the original image: the closer α is to one, the more important is the edge image.

Note that the three proposed measures have a dynamic range of $[-1, 1]$. The closer the value to 1, the higher the quality of the fused image.

4. Experimental Results

Assessing the performance of the quality measures for image fusion requires a calibrated set of subjective evaluations trials against which the proposed objective quality measures can be compared. Examples of such sets had been used in [23, 9] to validate some of the non-reference quality fusion measures presented in this chapter. Results showed that, for those given tests, gradient-based algorithms (such as [24]) and those based on SSIM (such as Q_W) corresponded much better to the subjective evaluations. Thus, these kind of measures can be useful to replace or assist subjective tests.

As illustration, we use the proposed fusion quality measures defined in (7), (8) and (9) to evaluate different multiresolution image fusion schemes. We do not, however, have a calibrated set of subjectives evalutations to compare with.

In the computation of the quality measures defined in last section, we take $\lambda(w)$ as in (6), with $s(x_A|w)$, $s(x_B|w)$ being the variance of images x_A and x_B, respectively, within the window w of size 8×8. In all displayed images, we have performed a histogram stretching and we have scaled the gray values of the pixels between 0 (black) and 255 (white).

4.1. Case Studies

In the next two experiments, we present some results using the Laplacian pyramid, the ratio pyramid and the spatially-invariant discrete wavelet transform (SIDWT) as multiresolution transforms of the input sources. In all cases we perform a 3-level decomposition. We combine the coefficients of the multiresolution decompositions of each input by selecting at each position the coefficient with a maximum absolute value, except for the approximation coefficients from the lowest resolution where we take the average. For comparison, we also use the simple fusion method of averaging the input images.

Case 1. Fusion of Complementary Blurred Images - Figure 1

First, we take as input images the complementary pair shown in the top row of Figure 1. They have been created by blurring the original 'Cameraman' image of size 256×256 with a disk of diameter of 11 pixels. The images are complementary in the sense that the blurring occurs at the left half and the right half, respectively. In the second row we display their total weights used to compute Q_W in (8). More specifically, each pixel (m, n) in the left image contains the value $c(w)\lambda(w)$ with w being the window whose top-left corner corresponds to (m, n). Similarly, the right image displays $c(w)\big(1 - \lambda(w)\big)$ for every $w \in W$. The fused images obtained by the Laplacian pyramid, the ratio pyramid, the SIDWT and the average are depicted in the third and fourth row, from left to right. Table 1 compares the quality of these fused images using our proposed quality measures. The first row corresponds to the fusion quality measure Q defined in (7), the second row to the weighted fusion quality measure Q_W in (8) and the third row to the edge-dependent fusion quality measure Q_E in (9) with $\alpha = 1/2$. For comparison, we also compute the l^2-metric in (1) between the original 'Cameraman' image and each of the fused images. Note that in 'real' fusion scenarios we do not have access to the original image. The resulting errors are shown in the last row of Table 1. Figure 1 shows that the Laplacian and SIDWT methods are comparable and that they outperform the other two schemes. Note, for instance, the blurring (e.g., in the buildings) and the loss of texture (e.g., in the grass) of the fused images obtained by the ratio pyramid and averaging. Furthermore, in the ratio-pyramid fused image, the details of the man's face have been cleared out, and in the average fused image, the loss of contrast is evident. These subjective visual comparisons are corroborated by the results in Table 1. Note that the Laplacian method has a higher Q_E than the SIDWT. This is most likely due to the fact that the former method is better able to preserve edges and reduce the ringing artifacts around them.

Table 1. Comparison between different quality measures for the fused images in Figure 1

measure	Laplacian	Ratio	SIDWT	Average
Q	0.903	0.764	**0.930**	0.830
Q_W	0.962	0.827	**0.965**	0.874
Q_E	**0.966**	0.781	0.962	0.689
d_2	**8.41**	164.35	13.03	30.66

Case 2. Fusion of a Magnetic Resonance Image (MRI) and a Computer Tomography (CT) Image - Figure 2

Consider now the input images in the top row of Figure 2. We repeat the same computations as described above. The results are shown in Figure 2 and Table 2. In this case, however, as we do not have a reference image to compare with, we cannot compute the l^2-metric. Instead, we use a measure based on mutual information. More precisely, the results in the last row of Table 2 have been obtained by adding the mutual information between the fused image and each of the inputs, such as in (3), and dividing it by the sum of the entropies of the inputs, i.e.,

$$\mathrm{MI}(x_A, x_B, x_F) = \frac{I(x_A; x_F) + I(x_B; x_F)}{H(x_A) + H(x_B)}.$$

Figure 1. Case 1. Top: input images x_A (left) and x_B (right). Second row: total weights $c \cdot \lambda$ (left) and $c \cdot (1 - \lambda)$ (right). Third row: fused images with a Laplacian (left) and a ratio (right) pyramid decompositions. Bottom: fused images with a SIDWT (left) decomposition and averaging (right).

In this way, we normalize the measure in (3) to the range $[0, 1]$.

In Figure 2, we can see that again the Laplacian and SIDWT methods clearly outperform the other two methods. For both of them, many details (specially the brain tissue in the magnetic resonance image) have been lost. Moreover, due to the high contrast in the input images, the ratio pyramid blows up the dynamic range for some pixels, which makes it necessary to clip them in order to be able to 'visualize' the image. Again, the subjective visual analysis is consistent with

Table 2. Comparison between different quality measures for the fused images in Figure 2

measure	Laplacian	Ratio	SIDWT	Average
Q	0.661	0.601	**0.699**	0.636
Q_W	**0.799**	0.673	0.770	0.642
Q_E	**0.834**	0.645	0.814	0.608
MI	0.337	0.221	0.409	**0.691**

the new quality indices, as shown in Table 2. In both experiments, the edge-dependent fusion quality measure gives a stronger separation between the good results (Laplacian and SIDWT) and the bad results (ratio and average). Note that the last row, where mutual information has been used, gives the best ranking to the average fusion method. However, mutual information has been shown to be a good indicator of the quality of multiresolution-based fused images [12] (as long as the average is not taken in all levels for the construction of the fused MR decomposition).

Conclusion

Objective performance assessment in fusion is largely an open problem and has received much attention in the last few years.

In this chapter, we have discussed some objective quality measures for image fusion which do not require a reference image and correlate well with subjective criteria as well as with other existing performance measures. These measures are easy to calculate and applicable to various input modalities (and hence to different fusion applications). In particular, they give good results on variable quality input images since they take into account the locations as well as the magnitude of the distortions.

There are several areas in which these quality measures can be extended. For example, considering color images [17]. Other visual mechanisms of our visual system may also be taken into account. One such mechanism is multiresolution. Since the sensitivity of the human visual system varies over spatial frequencies, it seems natural to compute the quality measures with respect to the scales of the objects that appear in the image [22]. Another possible extension is to include object or region information. Rather than calculating the quality measure in

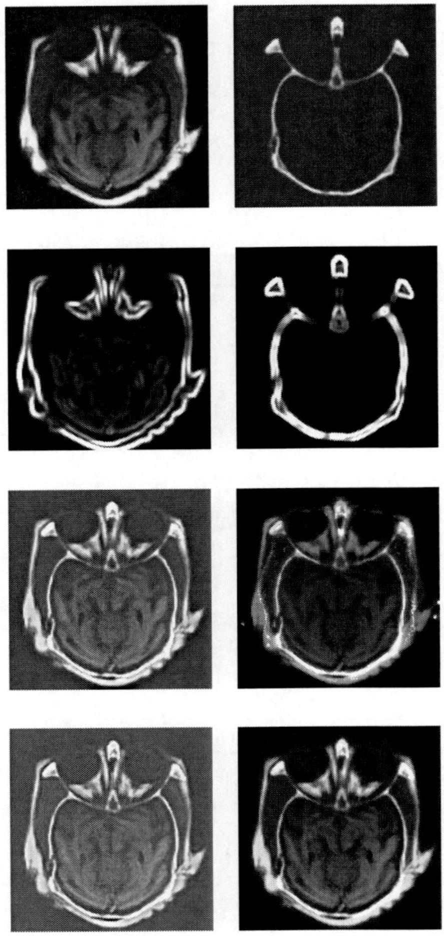

Figure 2. Case 2. Top: input images x_A (MRI, left) and x_B (CT image, right). Second row: total weights $c \cdot \lambda$ (left) and $c \cdot (1 - \lambda)$ (right). Third row: fused images with a Laplacian (left) and a ratio (right) pyramid decompositions. Bottom: fused images with a SIDWT (left) decomposition and averaging (right).

fixed windows, one might choose to segment the sources first and compute the measure region by region [11, 14].

Further research is also necessary to study the influence of the different parameters of the measures (e.g., size of the window, choice of saliency and weights, etc.), and how to select them in order to optimize the quality measures.

References

[1] Chen, H., and Varshney, P. K. A human perception inspired quality metric for image fusion based on regional information. *Information Fusion* 8, 2 (2007), 193 – 207.

[2] Chen, Y., and Blum, R. A new automated quality assessment algorithm for night vision image fusion. In *CISS '07, 41st Annual Conference on Information Sciences and Systems*, 2007 (March 2007), pp. 518–523.

[3] Cvejic, N., Łoza, A., Bull, D., and Canagarajah, N. A similarity metric for assessment of image fusion algorithms. *International Journal of Signal Processing* (2005).

[4] Hong, R., Cao, W., Pang, J., and Jiang, J. Directional projection based image fusion quality metric. *Information Sciences* 281, 10 (2014), 611 – 619.

[5] Huang, W., and Jing, Z. Evaluation of focus measures in multi-focus image fusion. *Pattern Recognition Letters* 28, 4 (2007), 493 – 500.

[6] Kotwal, K., and Chaudhuri, S. A bayesian approach to visualization-oriented hyperspectral image fusion. *Information Fusion* 14, 4 (2013), 349 – 360.

[7] Li, H., Manjunath, B. S., and Mitra, S. K. Multisensor image fusion using the wavelet transform. *Graphical Models and Image Processing* 57, 3 (May 1995), 235–245.

[8] Li, S., and Yang, B. Multifocus image fusion by combining curvelet and wavelet transform. *Pattern Recognition Letters* 29, 9 (2008), 1295 – 1301.

[9] Petrović, V. Subjective tests for image fusion evaluation and objective metric validation. *Information Fusion* 8, 2 (2007), 208–216.

[10] Petrović, V. and Dimitrijević, V. Focused pooling for image fusion evaluation. *Information Fusion* 22, 0(2015), 119, 126.

[11] Piella, G., and Heijmans, H. J. A. M. A new quality metric for image fusion. In *Proceedings of the IEEE International Conference on Image Processing* (Barcelona, Spain, September 14-17 2003).

[12] Qu, G. H., Zhang, D. L., and Yan, P. F. Information measure for performance of image fusion. *Electronic Letters* 38, 7 (2002), 313–315.

[13] Ryan, D., and Tinkler, R. Night pilotage assessment of image fusion. In *Helmet and Head-Mounted Displays and Symbology Design Requirements II* (Orlando, Florida, April 18-19 1995), Proceedings of SPIE, vol. 2465, pp. 50–67.

[14] Samadzadegan, F., and Javan, F. D. New object level strategy for image fusion quality assessment of high resolution satellite imagery. *International Journal of Image Processing* 27, 2 (2013), 140–148.

[15] Sheikh, H., and Bovik, A. Image information and visual quality. *IEEE Transactions on Image Processing* 15, 2 (Feb 2006), 430–444.

[16] Toet, A., and Franken, E. M. Perceptual evaluation of different image fusion schemes. *Displays* 24, 1 (February 2003), 25–37.

[17] Toet, A., and Lucassen, M. P. A new universal colour image fidelity metric. *Displays* 24, 45 (2003), 197 – 207.

[18] Wald, L., Ranchin, T., and Mangolini, M. Fusion of satellite images of different spatial resolutions: assessing the quality of resulting images. *Photogrammetric Engineering and Remote Sensing* 63, 3 (1997), 691–699.

[19] Wang, W., Jiao, L., and Yang, S. Fusion of multispectral and panchromatic images via sparse representation and local autoregressive model. *Information Fusion* 20, 0 (2014), 73 – 87.

[20] Wang, Z., and Bovik, A. A universal image quality index. *IEEE Signal Processing Letters* 9, 3 (March 2002), 81–84.

[21] Wang, Z., Bovik, A., Sheikh, H., and Simoncelli, E. Image quality assessment: from error visibility to structural similarity. *IEEE Transactions on Image Processing* 13, 4 (April 2004), 600–612.

[22] Wang, Z., Simoncelli, E. P., and Bovik, A. C. Multi-scale structural similarity for image quality assessment. In *Proc. IEEE Asilomar Conf. on Signals, Systems, and Computers, (Asilomar* (2003), pp. 1398–1402.

[23] Wielgus, M., and Putz, B. Comparative analysis of image fusion performance evaluation methods for the real-time environment monitoring system. In *Image Processing and Communications Challenges* 4. Springer Berlin Heidelberg, 2013, pp. 119–126.

[24] Xydeas, C., and Petrović, V. Objective pixel-level image fusion performance measure. In Sensor Fusion: Architectures, Algorithms and Applications IV (Orlando,Florida, April 24-28 2000), *Proceedings of SPIE*, vol. 4051, pp. 88–99.

[25] Yang, C., Zhang, J.-Q., Wang, X.-R., and Liu, X. A novel similarity based quality metric for image fusion. *Information Fusion* 9, 2 (April 2008), 156–160.

[26] Zhang, X. A novel quality metric for image fusion based on color and structural similarity. In *International Conference on Signal Processing Systems* (May 2009), pp. 258–262.

In: Image Fusion
Editor: C. T. Davis, pp. 17-43
ISBN: 978-1-63482-115-5

Chapter 2

Saliency Based Framework for Thermal and Visual Image Fusion

Ashirbani Saha[1,*], *Gaurav Bhatnagar*[2,†] *and Q. M. Jonathan Wu*[1‡]
[1]Department of Electrical and Computer Engineering,
University of Windsor, Ontario, Canada
[2]Centre for Information and Communication Technology,
Indian Institute of Technology, Jodhpur, India

Abstract

In this work, we propose an efficient framework for integrating or fusing thermal and visual images. This category of fusion finds application in navigation and surveillance systems. The main idea in this category of fusion is to successfully extract significant information from both of the thermal and visual images and combine them to form the fused image. The fused image has better representation of the entire scene as compared to the source images alone. Since, human beings are the principal judge of navigation and surveillance systems, we explore the ability of visual attention property of the human visual system (HVS) to generate the fused image. Generally, techniques for modeling the visual attention generate saliency maps in order to highlight the relative importance of pixels (or regions) in any image based on HVS. In the proposed approach, we use saliency maps from the source images to combine the significant thermal

*E-mail address: sahai@uwindsor.ca
†E-mail address: goravb@iitj.ac.in
‡E-mail address: jwu@uwindsor.ca

information with the significant visual information. The saliency maps serve two purposes. Firstly, they highlight the salient areas in the thermal and visual images. Secondly, the saliency values are also used to compute weights to generate the final fused image. Hence, the salient parts of the visual and thermal images are retained in the fused image. Different types of visual attention modeling techniques are used in the framework to demonstrate their relative performance in thermal and visual image fusion. Though the chosen modeling technique plays a key role in the performance of the fusion framework, our experiments on various image sets demonstrate the promise of the proposed approach in terms of visual inspection and different objective evaluation criteria. The novelty of the approach lies in developing a framework for saliency based fusion of thermal and visual information.

Keywords: image fusion, thermal images, image saliency, surveillance

1. Introduction

In general, a straightforward way to define image fusion is to merge 'effective' information from different source images to form a single image having equivalent 'effective' information of all the source images combined. The word 'effective' refers to the type of the information sought by the user from each image. Also, the nature of the source images may be different; for example, visual, thermal, different kinds of medical images and so on. Depending on the information sought and types of source images, several categories of image fusion have come into existence. In the present work, we chose to work on the fusion of visual and thermal images. Hence, the type of input or source images required for the fusion are different in nature. This kind of fusion aids or expands the ability of human vision by the integration of significant data which is otherwise invisible in visual images. The role of visual and thermal image fusion in surveillance and navigation has gained much importance in recent years [37]. In the areas of surveillance, this kind of fusion can aid in night-time vigilance [3] and concealed weapon detection [5]. For navigation and tracking, this fusion can improve the visual image in adverse weather conditions like smoke, fog, cloud (resulting in insufficient ambient light) [16] and night-time driving [34]. This type of fusion can also aid defect inspection [34] and human detection [10]. Due to its vast applicability, we make it our focus of discussion in this chapter. The present chapter is arranged as follows. In the remaining part of this section, we discuss the problems in thermal and visual image fusion along with the existing works in the area. In section 2, we explain the reasons for choosing image saliency to fuse visual and thermal images. Also, relevant image saliency detection techniques are discussed. The saliency based framework for fusion is discussed in details in section 3. The experiments, evaluation measures and performance analysis of the saliency based framework are conducted in section 4. Finally, section 5 presents the concluding remarks.

1.1. Basics of Thermal and Visual Image Fusion

The thermal image used as one of the sources in fusion captures the radiation emitted or reflected by the elements in the scene of inspection in the infrared range of the electromagnetic spectrum. The detail in the thermal image is expected to increase with the increase of thermal contrast among the elements of the scene. During night time and adverse weather conditions, targets can be better detected from the thermal image rather than the visual image. The thermal image is usually captured with infrared (IR) cameras. Depending on the operating frequency range, the output of the IR camera varies greatly. Hence, operating frequencies are varied based on the nature of the scene of inspection. On the other hand, visual images are captured by the cameras operating in the visual frequency range. The human visual system (HVS) is used to process visual image that can capture background details better than the thermal image acquisition system. At the same time, since visual cameras depend on ambient light, they fail to capture details pertaining to thermal contrast. Hence, by combining the important information (which are complementary in nature) from the thermal and visual images, the ability to inspect a scene gets better [38]. The images obtained from the visual and IR cameras need to be registered first to facilitate the fusion process which generates a single image having better information than each of the source images. There are a variety of techniques that have been developed over several years for this sort of fusion. The following discussion presents a synopsis of the existing literature in thermal and visual image fusion.

1.2. Existing Works in Thermal and Visual Image Fusion

Several approaches in the field of thermal and visual image fusion are present in literature. The approaches present a plethora of different avenues followed to achieve the same goal. The very basic technique for any kind of image fusion is the pixel level averaging [17], where the mean value of the corresponding pixels of the source images is used to represent the same pixel in the fused image. More sophisticated weighting techniques are given in Principal Component Analysis (PCA) based weighting [27] and Adaptive Weight Averaging (AWA) [18] methods. While the PCA based weighting uses the eigen vector corresponding to the largest eigen value of each source image, the AWA based method performs the fusion of IR and visual images by weights decided according to the local variance. One of the fundamental operations used in thermal and visual image processing is to generate the fused image by simply representing each of its pixels by the maximum of the value of the corresponding pixels in the source images. This is essentially the assignment of full weight to the maximum valued pixel and zero weight to the other.

Another approach uses the multiscale processing of the source images to generate the final fused image. In this approach, the first step is obtaining the pyramidal structure after the forward multiscale decomposition of both of the source images. Then, the activity level of the co-efficient is determined based on the pixel or window based or region based processing. Next, based on the activity level, the composite pyramidal structure of the fused image is formed. Finally, reverse multiscale decomposition is applied to this structure to obtain the fused image [5]. There are several techniques existing in this genre. Contrast Pyramid [39], Gradient Pyramid [8, 25], Discrete Wavelet Transform (DWT) [19, 41, 26, 12], Wavelet Packet Transform [2] and more recently Framelet Transform [3]. These methods differ in the type of multiscale transform chosen and the type of activity level measure. Also, some of them apply different strategies to high frequency and low frequency subbands. Apart from the multiscale transforms, other transforms like Fourier Transform [29], PCA [9], Independent Component Analysis (ICA) [24] and Discrete Cosine Transform (DCT) [33, 13] are used for the fusion. The processing steps using each of these transforms vary and cannot be unified to present a common strategy.

Another approach uses the statistical estimation theory to generate the fused image from the source images. The composite image is estimated by the probability models formed using the source images. In this regard, Gaussian Mixture Model (GMM) [4], Markov Random Field (MRF) [42] and Hidden Markov Model (HMM) [6] based techniques exist in the literature. Apart from the aforementioned approaches, learning based approaches are used involving neural networks [28] and more recently, sparse representation [44].

2. Why Image Saliency?

Human beings have the ability to locate the most informative part of any image, while inspecting it. This also involves spontaneous detection of any part, region or object in an image such that it stands out from the rest of the image. This ability of HVS is called visual attention. Computational techniques for modeling visual attention are available [22] and generally, they come up with saliency maps indicating the relative importance of different regions in an image as per the human attention. Hence, saliency map obtained from any image would highlight the most important part or parts that stand-out from the image as per the HVS. Saliency models have been applied to visual images to extract maps for different purposes like image texture classification [23], feature extraction [31], image quality assessment [30], and more specific applications like yarn surface evaluation [20]. However, computing saliency maps from thermal images is also beneficial as any interesting event in thermal image is likely to have a contrast difference with the remaining portion of the image. Since, contrast difference is an imminent factor in determining visual attention [15], saliency maps are likely to respond to this contrast difference. As an example, we show the saliency map in Fig. 1(b) obtained from the corresponding thermal image in Fig. 1(a) using the co-occurrence histogram based saliency computation method [22]. We will discuss all the images of the figure in detail after discussing all of the related saliency computation techniques. We discuss four saliency computation techniques which have been used in our saliency based framework. This discussion is necessary for the following reasons. First, it gives basic idea about generating the saliency maps in four fundamentally different ways. Second, it prepares a ground for explaining the performance of the saliency based framework using different types of saliency maps. The following four types of saliency map extraction techniques are chosen as they widely differ in their working principles and present comparative yet different saliency maps from each other.

2.1. Color Co-occurrence Histogram Based Saliency

The technique is proposed by Lu and Kim [22] and it uses color co-occurrence histograms to derive the saliency map. Co-occurrence histograms capture the local variation of intensity for each intensity value present in the image. Therefore, information regarding the discontinuity between object and image region is captured. In this technique, the normalized co-occurrence histogram is extracted separately from the three color channels of the image. Then, the average value of the co-occurrence histogram for each channel is calculated. The values above the corresponding average in each channel are considered to form the saliency map for that channel. Ultimately, the saliency maps for the three channels are averaged to obtain the final saliency map. As most of the thermal images are grayscale, saliency map from the only channel is available for a grayscale image. Thus, this way of finding saliency map relies on the rarity of intensity co-occurrence.

2.2. Graph Based Visual Saliency

Graph-based Visual Saliency [14] (GBVS) relies on extracting features from the images as per the human attention or fixation. The feature map is formed by linear filtering using Gabor filters followed by non-linear filtering. Then, a Markovian approach considering the distance or dissimilarity between regional feature values is used to form an activation map. Finally, normalization of the activation map takes place according to another Markovian process depending on the higher activation map values to obtain the saliency map.

2.3. Image Signature Based Saliency

This technique of saliency detection is proposed by Hou et al [15]. They proposed a feature called image signature (ISIG) derived from the sign of the DCT coefficients obtained from the image. Based on theoretical arguments, they showed that the feature can approximate the spatial location of a foreground hidden in a background, with the conditions that the foreground is sparse and the background is spectrally sparse. They experimentally demonstrate that the foreground location identified by image signature is consistent enough with the ground truth human eye fixation data over several images.

2.4. Frequency Tuned Saliency

Frequency tuned saliency [1] (FTS) is targeted to generate the saliency map by appropriate use of the frequency range. Low level features like color and luminance are used to generate the saliency maps. The features are extracted by the Difference-of-Gaussians (DOG) filter. The variances of the Gaussian filters are carefully chosen to retain high frequency content properly. The saliency map obtained by this process has well defined object boundaries compared to the other methods discussed earlier and several other techniques present in the literature. To generate a saliency map using this method for our work, only a single channel is available for use.

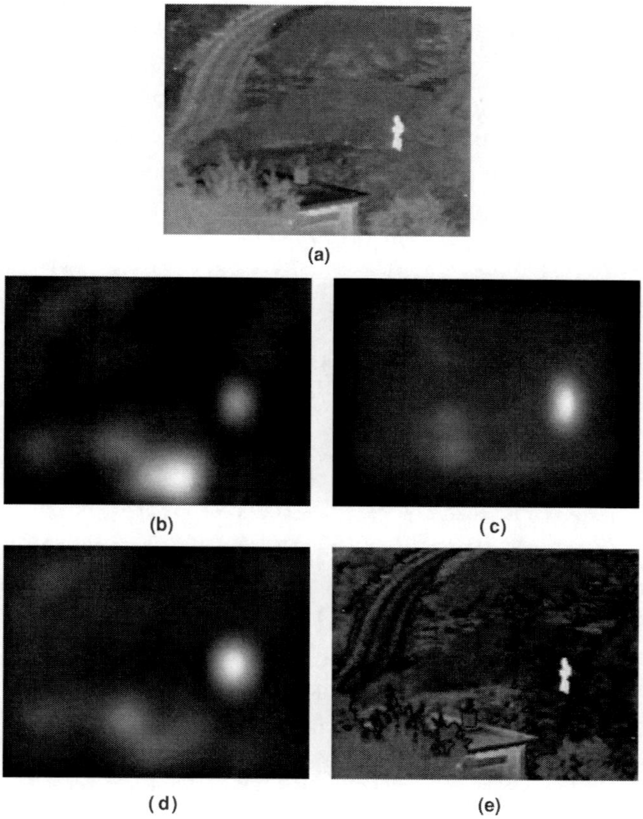

Figure 1. Saliency maps obtained for a thermal image shown in (a) using different techniques: (b) co-occurrence histogram based saliency (c) graph based visual saliency (d) image signature based saliency and (e) frequency tuned saliency.

2.5. Analysis of the Saliency Map

We are now able to analyze the saliency maps shown in Figs. 1(b)-(e) obtained by the respective techniques from the image in Fig. 1(a). We find that in Fig. 1(b), the maximum intensity is obtained at the corner of the roof of the house. This is due to the fact that the co-occurrence histogram based saliency relies on variations in neighborhood intensities and corner of the house is different from the neighboring regions. Also, the next high intensity is shown for the man in the image. High values of saliency corresponding to the man are also obtained for the GBVS and ISIG as shown in the Figs. 1(c) and (d), though the rest of the portions these two saliency maps are different. The FTS technique, on the other hand, assigns importance to the outlines of objects and hence the differences between objects are made much clear as shown in Fig. 1(e). In course of this, it is also able to assign high intensity to the man in the image. This result is in keeping with their results reported in [1].

The purpose to integrate the visual and thermal image is to aid the human observer for a better representation of the important information from both of the source images to improve the 'situational awareness' [38]. Hence, saliency maps from both of the images are likely to improve the visual interpretation of a given scene.

3. Saliency Based Fusion Framework

Based on our discussion in the section above, we design a saliency based framework for the fusion of thermal and visual images. The aim is to capture important information from the source images I_T (thermal image) and I_V (visual image). An important feature of thermal and visual image fusion is that the source information gathered from different sensors often lack necessary redundancy [5, 32]. Simple averaging or taking maximum of two sources at a pixel is likely to give an improved fused image [32]. However, a weighting scheme based on image saliency needs to be explored as it aims to combine the significant information from the sources as per HVS. In this section, we discuss the saliency based framework for image fusion. The block diagram of the framework is presented in Fig. 2. Saliency maps S_T and S_V, which are of the same dimension as the source images, are extracted from source images I_T and I_V respectively. Also, the saliency maps are normalized between the values of 0 and 1. With these saliency maps, we have the salient regions from both of the images in our grasp. Now, in order to generate the fused images, following steps are implemented. First, the saliency maps S_T and S_V are compared. For each pixel i, the maximum of $S_T(i)$ and $S_V(i)$ is computed to form $S_M(i)$. Thus,

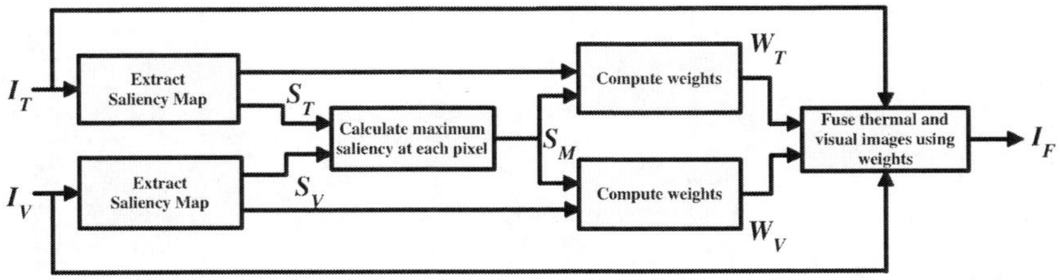

Figure 2. Block diagram of saliency based framework.

$S_M(i) = \max(S_T(i), S_V(i))$. Next, the following weights are computed

$$W_T(i) = \frac{S_T(i)}{S_M(i)}, \quad W_V(i) = \frac{S_V(i)}{S_M(i)} \tag{1}$$

It is apparent from the aforesaid equations that the maximum value of $W_T(i)$ or $W_V(i)$ can be 1 depending on the source of the $S_M(i)$. Therefore, unless the minimum of the two saliency values at pixel i is 0, the weights $W_T(i)$ and $W_V(i)$ are both non-zero. Also, we find that either of $W_T(i)$ and $W_V(i)$ will be 1, when $S_T(i) \neq S_V(i)$. The fused image is computed as

$$I_F(i) = \frac{W_T(i)I_T(i) + (1 - W_T(i))\, I_V(i) + W_V(i)I_V(i) + (1 - W_V(i))\, I_T(i)}{2} \tag{2}$$

Thus, the equation shows unless any of the weights is zero, the fused image pixel is composed of the weighted combination of the corresponding pixels from of both of the images. For analysis, if $W_T(i) = 1$ and $W_T(i) \neq W_V(i)$, $I_F(i) = \frac{I_T(i)+W_V(i)I_V(i)+(1-W_V(i))I_T(i)}{2}$. This implies that $I_T(i)$ is weighted higher than 0.5 and $I_V(i)$ is weighted less than 0.5. This is reasonable as thermal image for pixel i is weighted more due to its higher saliency. Also, based on $W_V(i)$, $I_T(i)$ can be of significant higher weight compared to $I_V(i)$ in this case. Hence, the majority of the contribution is obtained using the pixel values from that source image with higher value of saliency. If the saliency values from both of the images are close, the composite pixel value tends towards the higher of the pixel values in the source images. Hence, the fused image is combined of the important information from the thermal and visual images, as desired. The framework when used with co-occurrence histogram based saliency, is called Fusion_CH. It is also called Fusion_GBVS, Fusion_ISIG and Fusion_FTS when used with graph based visual saliency, image signature based saliency and frequency tuned saliency respectively. The fused image generated

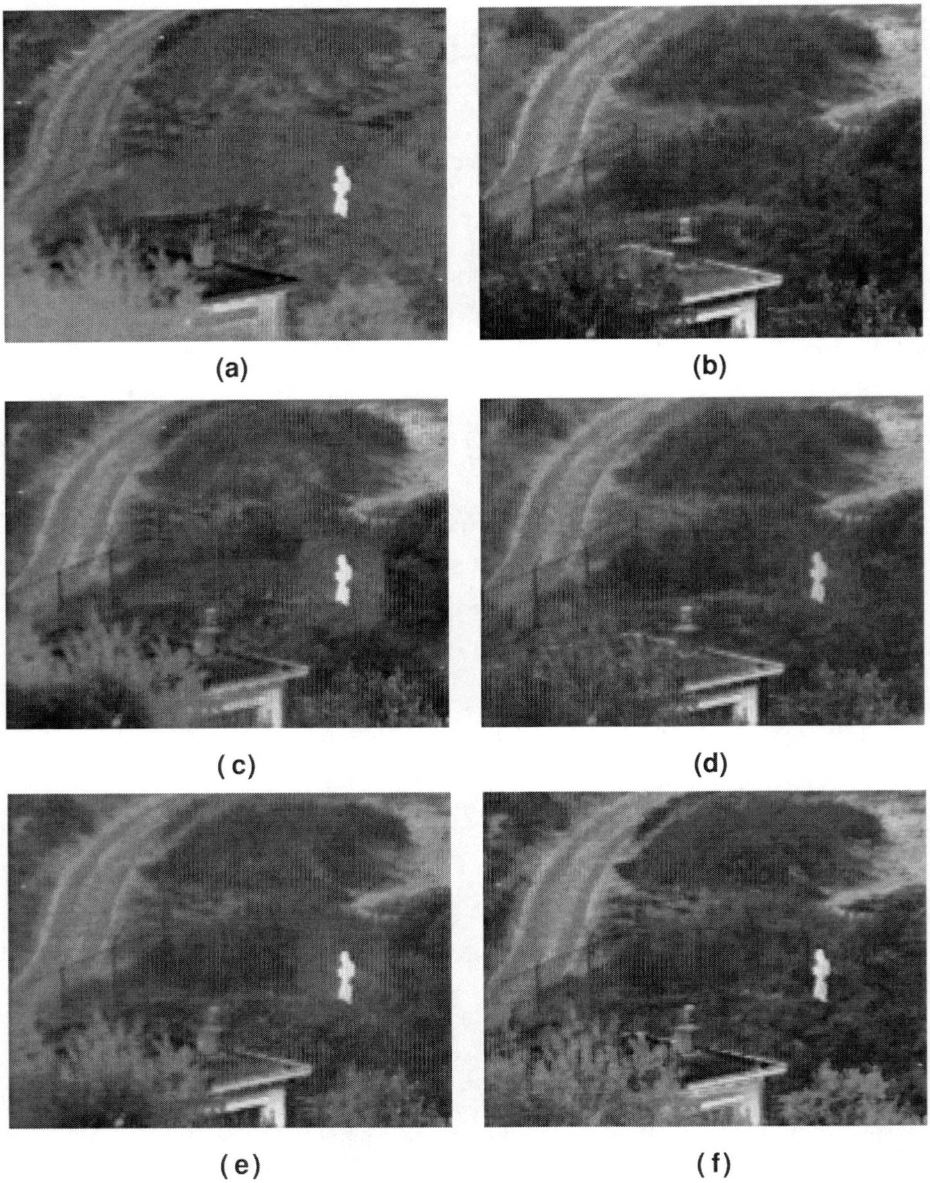

Figure 3. Results with framework for image set 1: (a) thermal image and (b) visual image. The fused images given by our framework are shown in next four images using (c) Fusion_CH (d) Fusion_GBVS (e) Fusion_ISIG and (f) Fusion_FTS (source image size : 360×270).

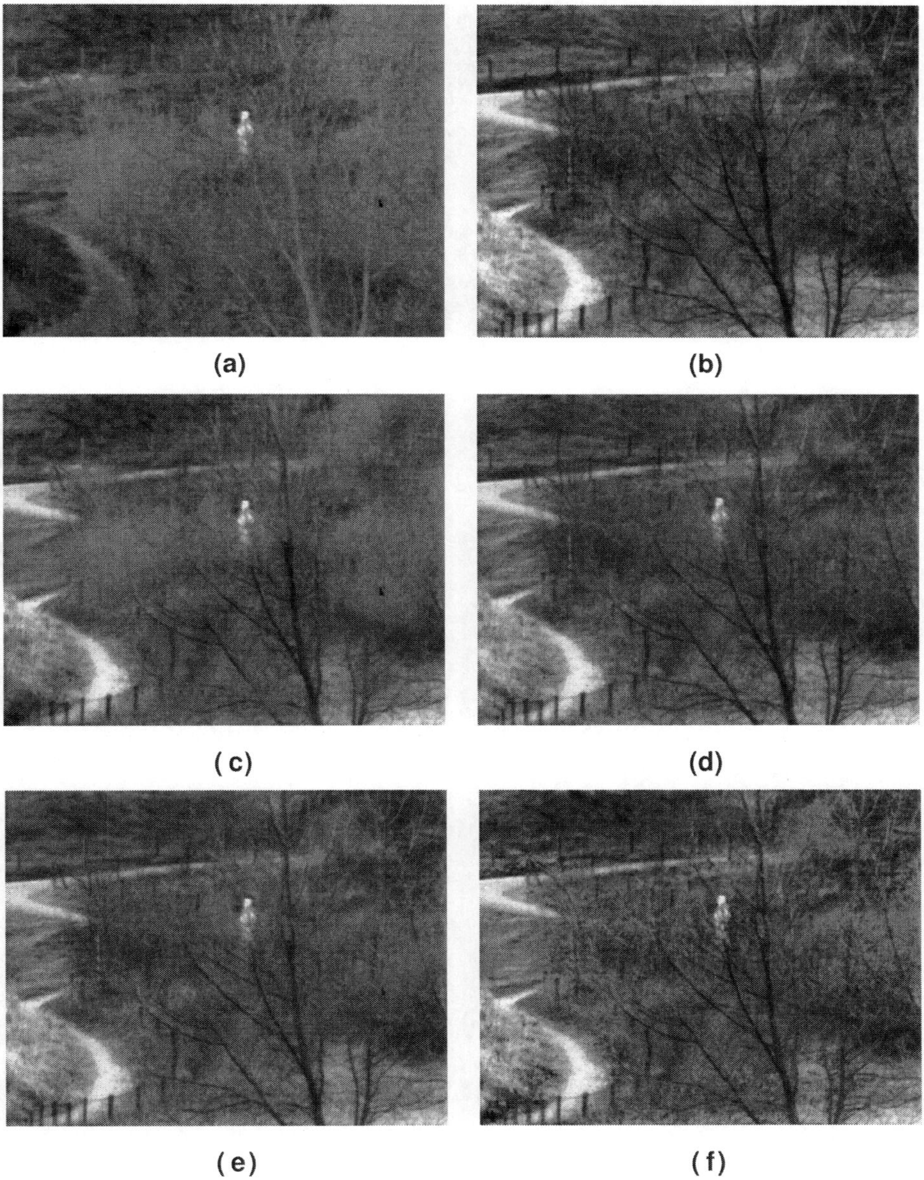

Figure 4. Results with framework for image set 2: (a) thermal image and (b) visual image. The fused images given by our framework are shown in next four images using (c) Fusion_CH (d) Fusion_GBVS (e) Fusion_ISIG and (f) Fusion_FTS (source image size : 360×300).

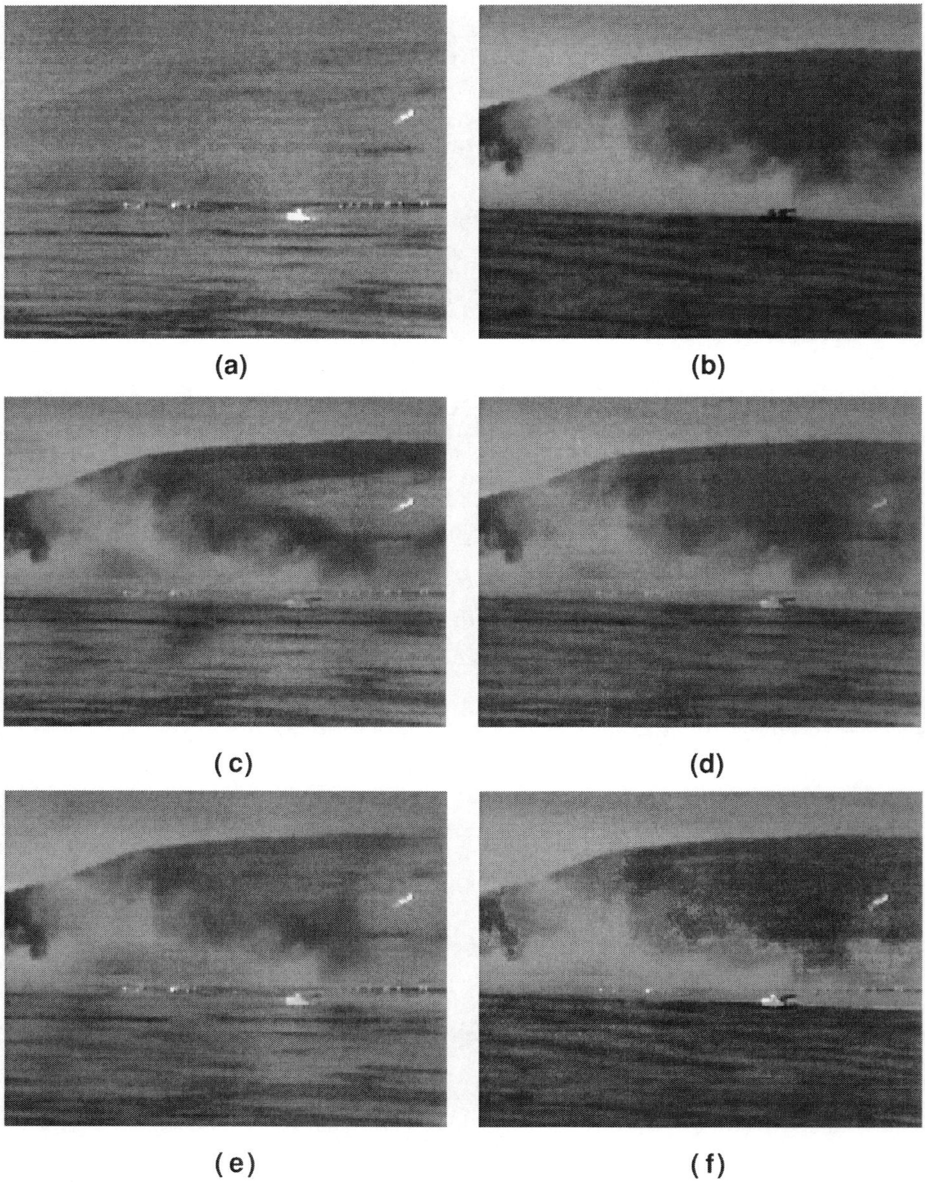

Figure 5. Results with framework for image set 3: (a) thermal image and (b) visual image. The fused images given by our framework are shown in next four images using (c) Fusion_CH (d) Fusion_GBVS (e) Fusion_ISIG and (f) Fusion_FTS (source image size : 240×180).

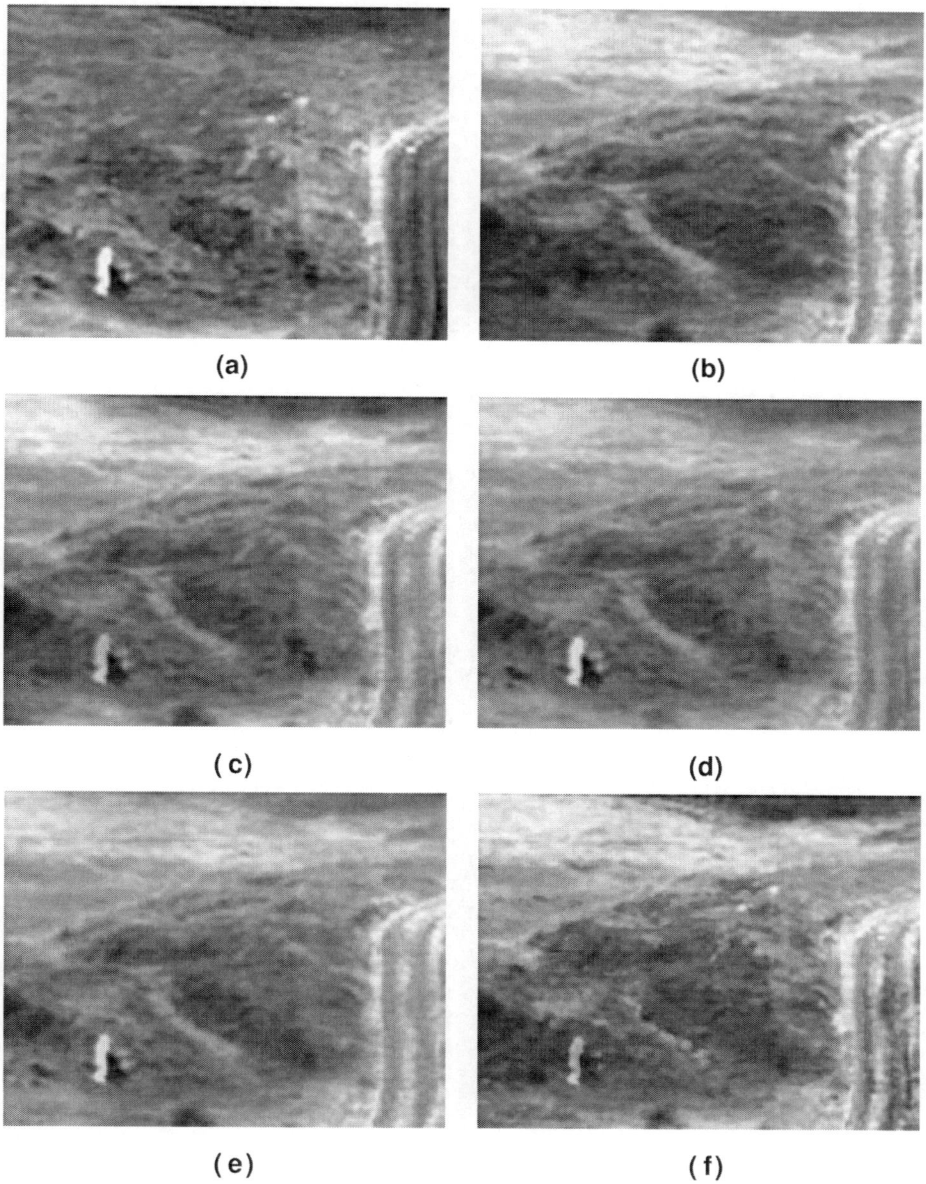

Figure 6. Results with framework for image set 4: (a) thermal image and (b) visual image. The fused images given by our framework are shown in next four images using (c) Fusion_CH (d) Fusion_GBVS (e) Fusion_ISIG and (f) Fusion_FTS (source image size : 360×240).

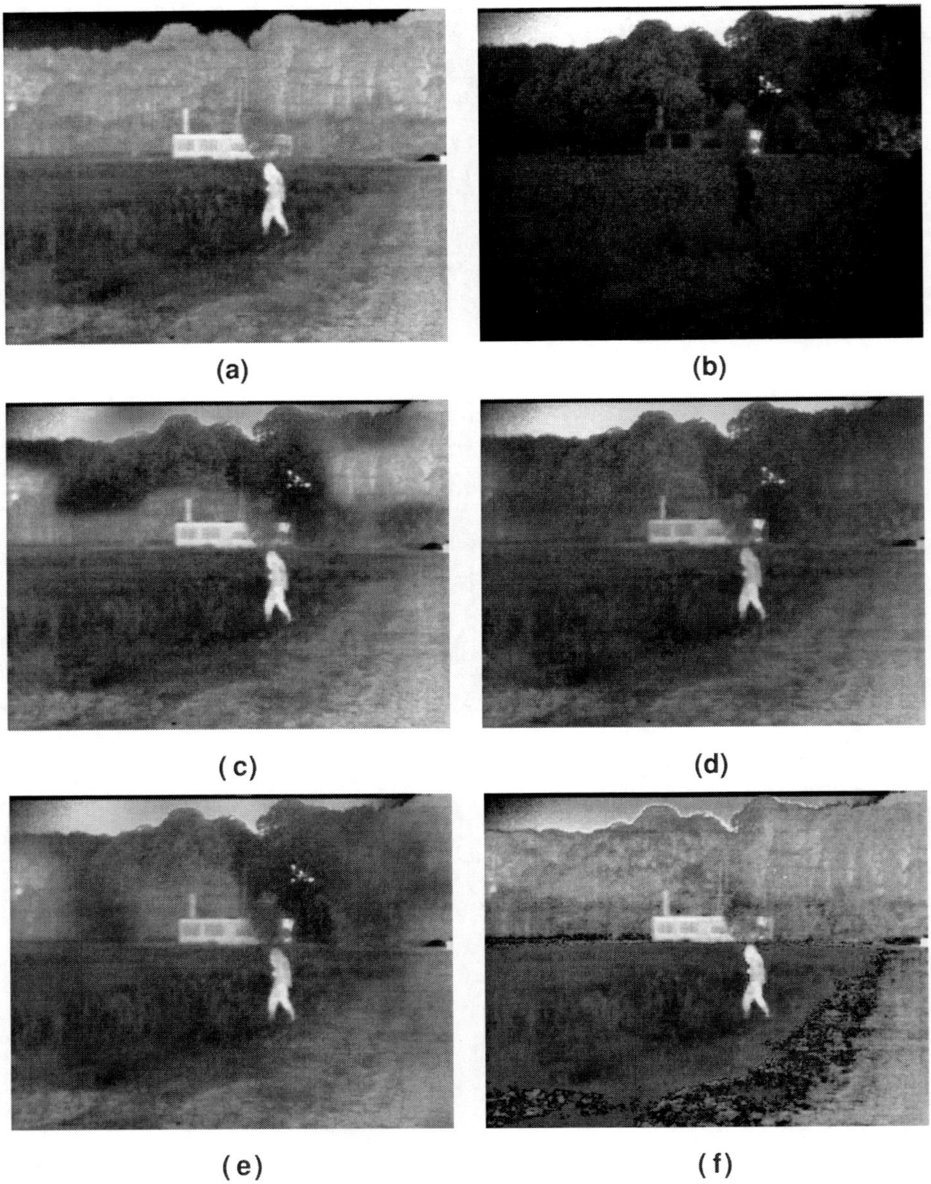

Figure 7. Results with framework for image set 5: (a) thermal image and (b) visual image. The fused images given by our framework are shown in next four images using (c) Fusion_CH (d) Fusion_GBVS (e) Fusion_ISIG and (f) Fusion_FTS (source image size : 360×240).

using the saliency based fusion framework is shown in Fig. 3. All of the thermal and visual image sets used in this work are taken from TNO-UN Camp database [35, 36] of surveillance images from TNO Human Factors provided by A. Toet. The fused images for image set 1 using the saliency based framework are shown in Fig. 3. Apart from the intruder showed in one of the source images, the background information about the fences is also brought forward by saliency based techniques. In Fig. 4, the intruder is shown in the thermal image but the background information about the intruder consisting of the branches of the trees, the path and fences are shown in the visual images. The fused images are able to combine all of these together. In Fig. 5, in spite of the haze in the visual image, certain objects are found in the thermal image. In the fused image, the framework is able to combine the mountain, haze and all the required objects. In Fig. 6, the contour of the sand dune is visible in the visual image, but the intruder can be seen in the thermal image only. The framework can combine all of this information together in the fused image. In Fig. 7, the human and the bus present in the thermal image can be easily identified in the fused images. In spite of the visual evidence of the effectiveness of the framework, a qualitative analysis is required to understand the comparative strengths of the saliency based techniques and several existing techniques in the literature.

4. Experimental Results

In this section, we present the experiments and results obtained using the saliency based framework. As we have already presented the visuals of the fused images using different saliency extraction techniques for five image sets (Figs. 3-7), the rest of this section discusses two aspects. Firstly, the definitions and effectiveness of the qualitative measures used to evaluate the quality of the fused image are discussed. Secondly, a comparative study of the saliency based framework is carried out against eight existing techniques in the literature.

4.1. Evaluation Measures

The evaluation procedure followed for the comparison of the proposed framework with the existing methods essentially amounts to evaluating the fused image irrespective of any ground truth. Several types of evaluation strategies have been used in different works [21, 3, 5]. However, the work presented in [21] has highlighted the disadvantages of several of these strategies. Therefore, the evaluation measures are chosen based on their advantages indicated in different studies. Mostly, the aim has been to evaluate the fused image with measures that compare the fused image with the sources by computing the information transfer between them. The chosen evaluation measures are Cross Entropy, $Q^{I_T I_V/I_F}$ computed based on transmitted edge information and finally, the Image Fusion Performance Measure. The definitions of these measures are given below.

I. **Cross Entropy.** From the source images I_T and I_V and the fused image I_F, the cross entropy (C_E) is computed as follows:

$$C_E = \frac{\mathrm{E}_R(I_T, I_F) + \mathrm{E}_R(I_V, I_F)}{2} \tag{3}$$

where $\mathrm{E}_R(X, Y)$ is the function used to compute the relative entropy of the image X relative to the image Y as

$$\mathrm{E}_R(X, Y) = \sum_{i=0}^{L} p_X(i) \log_2 \frac{p_X(i)}{p_Y(i)}. \tag{4}$$

Here $p_X(i)$ is the normalized frequency of the intensity level i computed from the image X. The total number of intensity levels is $(L + 1)$. The value computed using the function $E_R(X, Y)$ is always non-negative [11] and becomes zero only when $X = Y$. The relative entropy of X with respect to Y gives a physical idea about the excess number of bits (in this case, excess information) required to infer about the distribution of X when that of Y is given instead of X. Therefore, smaller value of C_E indicates that less amount of excess information is required to infer about the source images when the fused image is available. In turn, this signifies that fused image has more of the information from the source images. However, it is shown in [21] that presence of noise makes it difficult to evaluate with C_E. Hence, we have used two more measures for the evaluation.

II. $\boldsymbol{Q^{I_T I_V/I_F}}$**.** This edge based similarity measure gives the similarity between the edges transferred in the fusion process [43]. Mathematically, $Q^{I_T I_V/I_F}$ is defined as

$$Q^{I_T I_V/I_F} = \frac{\sum_{i=1}^{M} \left[Q_i^{I_T I_F} w_i^T + Q_i^{I_V I_F} w_i^V \right]}{\sum_{i=1}^{M} \left[w_i^T + w_i^V \right]}. \tag{5}$$

where I_T, I_V and I_F represent the sources and the fused image respectively. The weights w_i^T and w_i^V are computed using the edge strength. The definition of $Q_i^{I_T I_F}$ and $Q_i^{I_V I_F}$ are same and given as

$$Q_i^{I_T I_F} = Q_{g,i}^{I_T I_F} Q_{\alpha,i}^{I_T I_F}, \quad Q_i^{I_V I_F} = Q_{g,i}^{I_V I_F} Q_{\alpha,i}^{I_V I_F}. \tag{6}$$

such that $Q_{g,i}^{I_T I_F}$ and $Q_{\alpha,i}^{I_T I_F}$ are the edge strength and orientation preservation values at pixel i respectively from the source image I_T to fused image I_F. The dynamic range for $Q^{I_T I_V / I_F}$ is [0,1] and it should be as close to 1 as possible for better fusion, with 1 indicating the perfect fusion.

III. **Image Fusion Performance Measure (IFPM).** IFPM [40] is defined as

$$\text{IFPM} = \frac{C_I(I_F, I_T, I_V)}{H(I_T, I_V)} \tag{7}$$

The numerator $C_I(I_F, I_T, I_V)$ is representative of the total mutual information between the sources and fused image. It is calculated as

$$C_I(I_F, I_T, I_V) = I(I_T; I_F) + (I_V; I_F | I_T). \tag{8}$$

The first term in the aforesaid equation computes the mutual information between I_T and I_F. The second term computes the conditional mutual information of I_V and I_F when I_T is given. Thus, this second term is a measure of the information shared between I_V and I_F only. The denominator in Eqn. 7, is the joint entropy of the source images and hence a measure of the information conveyed by all the source images together. When the fused image conveys the same information as all the source images together, IFPM equals 1 indicating perfect fusion. Thus, IFPM values lie between 0 and 1 and higher values indicate better fusion.

4.2. Comparison with Existing Approaches

The comparison of the proposed framework is carried out using the aforementioned evaluation measures. The proposed framework is used with four saliency methods already discussed earlier. Hence, we compare Fusion_CH, Fusion_GBVS, Fusion_ISIG and Fusion_FTS with the existing techniques which include averaging [17], contrast pyramid [39], DWT [19], gradient pyramid [8], laplacian pyramid [7], selecting maximum valued pixel [17], morphological pyramid [12] and PCA [27]. The results using Cross Entropy are presented in Fig. 8 for five image sets. For image sets 1 and 4, the lowest C_E is obtained by the Fusion_CH. Fusion_FTS obtains the least C_E for image sets 3 and 5. For image set 2, the contrast pyramid performs better than the others. The saliency based framework has competitive or better performance than the other techniques as shown in the graphs. Thus, in terms of transmitting information from the sources to the fused image, the saliency based framework is effective considering C_E.

As we compare using $Q^{I_T I_V / I_F}$ in Fig. 9, except for image set 2, maximum value based fusion performs better than the rest. In image set 2, Fusion_GBVS is the best performer. Hence, in terms of transmission of edge based information the saliency based framework is effective, though several other methods of equivalent or higher effectiveness exist.

The comparison results using IFPM is presented in Fig. 10. This experiment shows that Fusion_FTS performs much better than the Fusion_CH, Fusion_GBVS and Fusion_ISIG. For image sets 3 and 4, it performs better than the rest of the methods. For image sets 1 and 2, PCA based weighting is the best performer and selecting maximum valued pixel based fusion performs best for image set 5.

We have presented a comprehensive evaluation of the proposed method with three evaluation measures. However, we find that it is difficult to interpret and draw a comprehensive conclusion in this way. Hence, we present a ranking methodology based on the three measures. For each image set and a performance evaluation measure, we rank all the measures from 1 to 12. For example, fusion techniques having lower C_E have lower ranking since lower values of C_E indicate better fusion. In contrast, fusion techniques having higher values of $Q^{I_T I_V / I_F}$ (or IFPM) are ranked lower since higher values of $Q^{I_T I_V / I_F}$ (or IFPM) indicate better fusion. Hence, lower rank will always indicate a better measure for efficient fusion. Now, for all of the techniques, we take the mean for all of their ranks over different image sets and evaluation measures. As shown in Table 1, the final rank assigned to each measure is based on sorting their mean ranks in ascending order. The fusion technique with the lowest rank is Fusion_CH and that with the highest rank is gradient pyramid based technique. These ranks are dependent on the type of fusion, fusion technique used, image sets considered for testing as well as the performance evaluation measures considered. Though the techniques based on our saliency framework are simple and linear way of generating the fused image, Fusion_CH and Fusion_FTS perform better than several existing techniques in the literature.

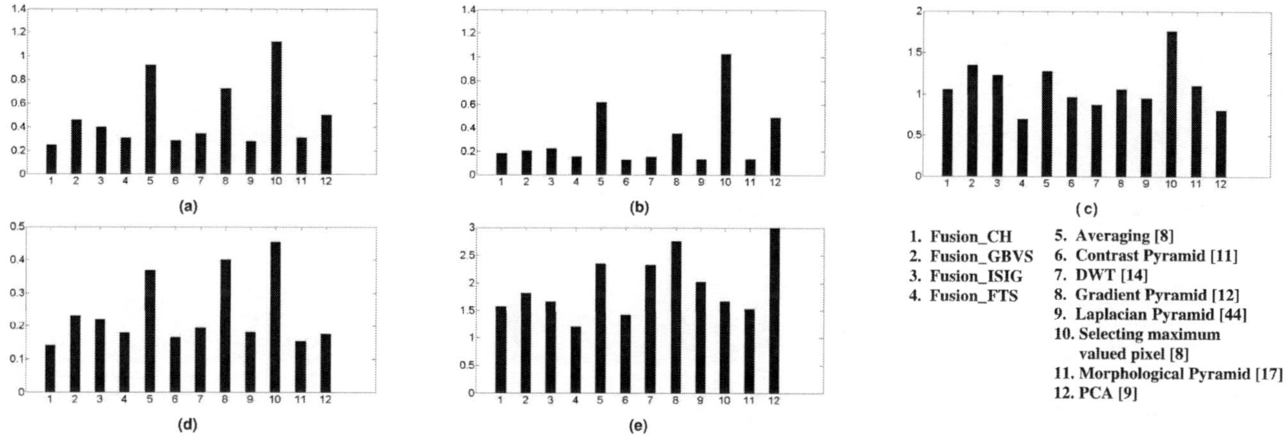

Figure 8. Comparison of the saliency based fusion techniques (shown along the x-axis, names of the techniques are shown in the legend) with existing techniques using Cross Entropy (shown along the y-axis). (a), (b), (c), (d) and (e) enlist the comparison results for image sets 1, 2, 3, 4 and 5 respectively.

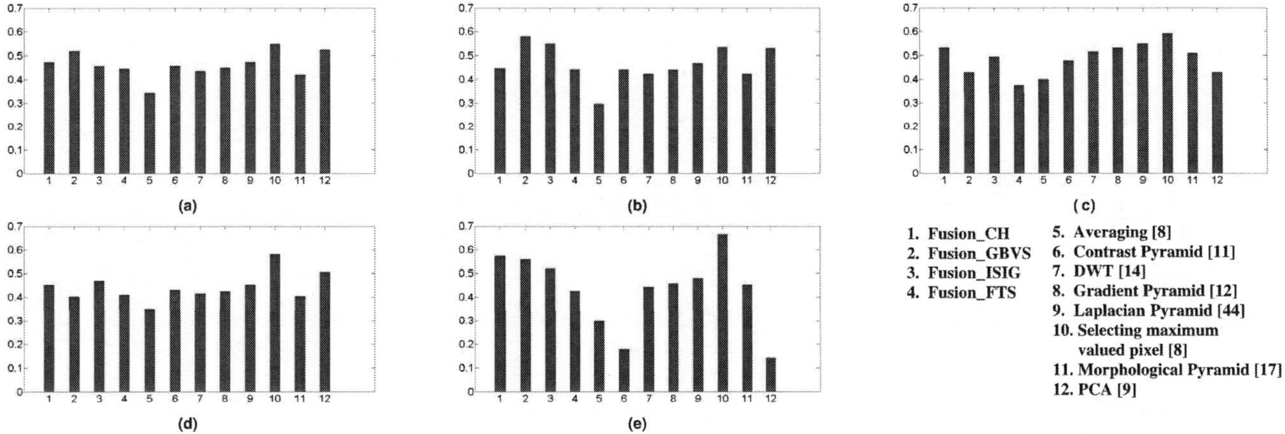

Figure 9. Comparison of the saliency based fusion techniques (shown along the x-axis, names of the techniques are shown in the legend) with existing techniques using $Q^{I_T I_V / I_F}$ (shown along the y-axis). (a), (b), (c), (d) and (e) enlist the comparison results for image sets 1, 2, 3, 4 and 5 respectively.

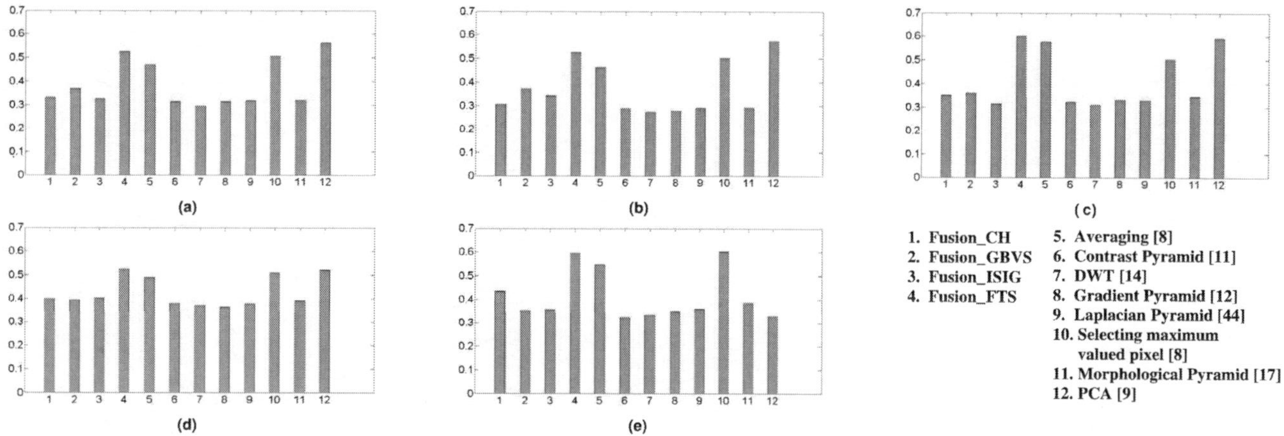

Figure 10. Comparison of the saliency based fusion techniques (shown along the x-axis, names of the techniques are shown in the legend) with existing techniques using IFPM (shown along the y-axis). (a), (b), (c), (d) and (e) enlist the comparison results for image sets 1, 2, 3, 4 and 5 respectively.

Table 1. Final ranking of different fusion techniques

Method	Ranking
Fusion_CH	1
Fusion_FTS	2
Selecting maximum valued pixel [17]	3
PCA [27]	4
Laplacian Pyramid [7]	5
Fusion_ISIG	6
Fusion_GBVS	7
Morphological Pyramid [12]	8
Contrast Pyramid [39]	9
Averaging [17]	10
DWT [19]	11
Gradient Pyramid [8]	12

Conclusion

This chapter presented a framework for the fusion of visual and thermal images. The framework relies on the theory of visual attention and shows that important information that can be detected by human eyes in thermal images can be indicated by saliency maps as well. Important information in visual images is detected by saliency maps, as indicated by earlier research. Hence, an effort is made to develop an image fusion framework based on saliency maps. These maps are used to form weights to linearly combine information from the source images.

Four different types of saliency map extraction techniques are applied to the framework to obtain four different versions of the same. The ability and effectiveness of the framework are demonstrated by its performance on a suite of different image sets. In order to quantitatively analyze the performance of the framework, three evaluation measures with respective benefits are used to compare the four versions with the existing techniques in the literature. The saliency based framework showed competitive performance with the existing techniques. Also, a procedure is used to combine the quantitative performance using all evaluation measures to assign a final rank to all the fusion techniques compared in this work. Two saliency based techniques are identified as the best approaches among the techniques compared using this methodology.

After demonstrating the effectiveness of the saliency based framework, the open question remains about the optimal way to use saliency maps to generate a fused image. An intuitive and reasonable approach is followed in this work to use saliency maps for fusing thermal and visual images. However, finding the optimal way to use the saliency maps for image fusion is a topic of further research and is left as a future work.

Acknowledgment

This work is supported in part by the Canada Research Chair Program and the Natural Sciences and Engineering Research Council of Canada.

References

[1] R. Achanta, S. Hemami, F. Estrada, and S. Susstrunk. Frequency-tuned salient region detection. In *IEEE International Conference on Computer Vision and Pattern Recognition*, pages 1597–1604, 2009.

[2] G. Bhatnagar and B. Raman. A new image fusion technique based on directive contrast. *Electronic Letters on Computer Vision and Image Analysis*, 8(2):18–38, 2009.

[3] G. Bhatnagar, Q. M. J. Wu, and B. Raman. Navigation and surveillance using night vision and image fusion. In *IEEE Symposium on Induatrial Electronics and Applications*, pages 342–347, 2011.

[4] R. S. Blum and J. Yang. Image fusion using the expectation maximization algorithm and a Gaussian mixture model. In G. L. Foresti, C. S. Regazzoni, and P.K. Varshney, editors, *Advanced Video-based Surveillance Systems*. Kluwer, Boston, 2003.

[5] R.S. Blum, Z. Xue, and Z. Zhang. An overview of image fusion. In *Multi-Sensor Image Fusion and Its Applications*, pages 1–38. Taylor & Francis, 2005.

[6] R.S. Blum and J. Yang. A statistical signal processing approach to image fusion using hidden markov models. In *Multi-Sensor Image Fusion and Its Applications*, pages 265–288. Taylor & Francis, 2005.

[7] P. J. Burt and E. H. Adelson. The Laplacian pyramid as a compact image code. *IEEE Transactions on Communications*, 31(4):532–540, 1983.

[8] P. J. Burt and R. J. Kolczynski. Enhanced image capture through fusion. In *International Conference on Computer Vision*, pages 173–182, 1993.

[9] P. S. Chavez and A. Y. Kwarteng. Extracting spectral contrast in landsat thematic mapper image data using selective principal component analysis. *Photogrammetric Engineering and Remote Sensing*, 55:339–348, 1989.

[10] E. J. Choi and D. J. Park. Human detection using image fusion of thermal and visible image with new joint bilateral filter. In *Computer Sciences and Convergence Information Technology*, pages 882–885, 2010.

[11] T. M. Cover and J. A. Thomas. *Elements of Information Theory*, chapter Entropy, Relative Entropy and Mutual Information. John Wiley & Sons, Inc., 1991.

[12] I. De and B. Chanda. A simple and efficient algorithm for multifocus image fusion using morphological wavelets. *Signal Processing*, 86(5):924–936, 2006.

[13] M. B. A. Haghighat, A. Aghagolzadeh, and H. Seyedarabi. Multi-focus image fusion for visual sensor networks in DCT domain. *Computers and Electrical Engineering*, 37(5):789–797, 2011.

[14] J. Harel, C. Koch, and P. Perona. Graph-based visual saliency. In *Advances in Neural Information Processing Systems* 19, pages 545–552, 2007.

[15] X. Hou, J. Harel, and C. Koch. Image signature : Highlighting sparse salienct regions. *IEEE Transactions on Pattern Analysis and Machine Intelligence*, 34(1):194–201, 2012.

[16] K.S.Kumar, G. Kavitha, R. Subramanian, and G. Ramesh. Visual and thermal image fusion for UAV based target tracking. In *MATLAB-A Ubiquitous Tool for the Practical Engineer*, pages 307–326. InTech, 2011.

[17] F. Laliberte and L. Gagnon. Studies on registration and fusion of retinal images. In *Multi-Sensor Image Fusion and Its Applications*, pages 1–38. Taylor & Francis, 2005.

[18] E. Lallier and M. Farooq. A real-time pixel level based image fusion via adaptive weight averaging. In *The Third International Conference on Information Fusion*, pages WeC3_3–WeC3_13, 2000.

[19] H. Li, B. S. Manjunath, and S. K. Mitra. Multisensor image fusion using the wavelet transform. *Graph Models Image Processing*, 57(3):235–245, 1995.

[20] Z. Liang, B. Xu, Z. Chi, and D. D. Feng. Relative saliency model over multiple images with an application to yarn surface evaluation. *IEEE Transactions on Cybernetics*, 44(8):1249–1258, 2014.

[21] S. Lu and J.-H. Lim. Experimental tests of image fusion for night vision. In *International Conference on Information Fusion*, pages 491–498, 2005.

[22] S. Lu and J.-H. Lim. Saliency modeling from image histograms. In *European Conference on Computer Vision, Lecture Notes in Computer Science*, volume 7578, pages 321–332, 2012.

[23] J. Melendez, D. Puig, and M. A. Garcia. Multi-level pixel-based texture classification through efficient prototype selection via normalization cut. *Pattern Recognition*, 43(12):4113–4123, 2010.

[24] N. Mitianoudis and T. Stathaki. Adaptive image fusion using ICA bases. In *IEEE Conference on Acoustics, Speech, and Signal Processing*, volume 2, pages 829–832, 2006.

[25] V. S. Petrovic and C. S. Xydeas. Gradient-based multiresolution image fusion. *IEEE Transactions on Image Processing*, 13(2):228–237, 2004.

[26] G. Piella. A general framework for multiresolution image fusion: from pixels to regions. *Information Fusion*, 4(4):259–280, 2003.

[27] O. Rockinger and T. Fechner. Pixel level image fusion : The case of image sequences. In *SPIE*, pages 378–388, 1998.

[28] R.P.Broussard, S. K. Rogers, M. E. Oxley, and G. L. Tarr. Physiologically motivated image fusion for object detection using a pulse coupled neural network. *IEEE Transactions on Neural Networks*, 10(3):554–563, 1999.

[29] A. Saha, G. Bhatnagar, and Q. M. J. Wu. Mutual spectral residual approach for multifocus image fusion. *Digital Signal Processing*, 23(4):1121–1135, 2013.

[30] A. Saha and Q. M. J. Wu. A study on using spectral saliency detection approaches for image quality assessment. In *IEEE Conference on Acoustics, Speech, and Signal Processing*, pages 1889–1893, 2013.

[31] C. Siagian and L. Itti. Rapid biologically-inspired scene classification using features shared with visual attention. *IEEE Transactions on Pattern Analysis and Machine Intelligence*, 29(2):300–312, 2007.

[32] S.R.Schnelle and A.L.Chan. Enhanced target tracking through infrared-visible image fusion. In *International Conference on Information Fusion*, pages 1962–1969, 2011.

[33] J. Tang. A contrast based image fusion technique in the DCT domain. *Digital Signal Processing*, 14(3), 2004.

[34] L. Tao, H. Ngo, M. Zhang, A. Livingston, and V. Asari. A multi-sensor image fusion and enhancement system for assisting drivers in poor lighting conditions. In *IEEE 34th Applied Imagery and Pattern Recognition Workshops*, pages 106–113, 2005.

[35] A. Toet. Detection of dim point targets in cluttered maritime backgrounds through multisensor image fusion. In *SPIE*, volume 4781, pages 118–129, 2002.

[36] A. Toet. Natural colour mapping for multiband nightvision imagery. *Information Fusion*, 4(3):155–166, 2003.

[37] A. Toet. Cognitive image fusion and assessment. In *Image Fusion*, pages 303–340. InTech, 2011.

[38] A. Toet, J. K. IJspeert, A. M. Waxman, and M. Aguilar. Fusion of visible and thermal imagery improves situational awareness. *Displays*, 18:85–95, 1997.

[39] A. Toet, L. J. Ruyven, and J. M. Valeton. Merging thermal and visual images by a contrast pyramid. *Optical Engineering*, 28:789–792, 1989.

[40] V. Tsagaris, N. Fragoulis, and C. Theoharatos. Performance evaluation of image fusion methods. In *Image Fusion*, pages 71–88. InTech, 2011.

[41] M. Unser. Texture classfication and segmentation using wavelet frames. *IEEE Transactions on Image Processing*, 4(9):1549–1560, 1995.

[42] W. A. Wright and F. Bristol. Quick Markov random field image fusion. In *SPIE*, volume 3374, pages 302–308, 1998.

[43] C. S. Xydeas and V. Petrovic. Objective pixel-level image fusion performance measure. In *SPIE, Sensor Fusion: Architectures, Algorithms, and Applications IV*, volume 4051, pages 89–98, 2002.

[44] Q. Zhang, Y. Fu, H. Li, and J. Zou. Dictionary learning method for joint sparse representation-based image fusion. *Optical Engineering*, 52(5):057006–1–057006–11, 2013.

In: Image Fusion
Editor: C. T. Davis, pp. 45-81
ISBN: 978-1-63482-115-5

Chapter 3

Fusion of Multifocus Color Images from Microscopic Samples Using the Modulus of the Gradient of the Color Planes

Carina Toxqui-Quitl**, *Román Hurtado-Pérez*, *Alfonso Padilla-Vivanco* and *Gabriel Ortega-Mendoza
Universidad Politécnica de Tulancingo, División de Ingenierías,
Calle Ingenierías, Tulancingo, Hidalgo, México

Abstract

Commonly in the light microscopy, the limited Depth-of-Field (DOF) of an imaging system causes blur images when the sample is wider than the DOF of the optical system. Additionally, the DOF decreases as the magnification increases. In order to extend the DOF of a microscopic system we propose a multifocus image fusion method based on the modulus of the gradient color planes. This procedure is applied to multi-focus microscopy color images which have been acquired by the bright-field reflection microscopy technique. Our results are obtained using real specimens and any post-processing step is done over the fused image. The proposed method is simple, fast and practically free of artifacts or false color.

*E-mail address: carina.toxqui@upt.edu.mx

PACS: 05.45-a, 52.35.Mw, 96.50.Fm

Keywords: Multifocus Image fusion, gradient color operator, depth of field, optical microscopy

AMS Subject Classification: 53D, 37C, 65P

1. Introduction

In general, focusing is a procedure of adjusting the distance between an optical system and its image plane until a contrast-enough image is reached. Focusing cameras is an important problem in computer vision and microscopy, due to the limited depth of field (*DOF*) of some optical systems. Particularly, images of thick objects acquired by using a microscope system are strongly blurred in the portion of the object that lies outside of the depth of field of the microscope objective lens. This means that, only small regions of the field of view are in-focus. In order to overcome this problem some techniques such as wavefront coding [1][2] and image fusion [3] [4] have been proposed.

Typically, many digital techniques have been proposed to generate fusion schemes. These fusion schemes are divided in (a) pixel-based image fusion [5], (b) neighborhood-based image fusion [6] and multiresolution image fusion [7][8]. It is well know that, image fusion schemes have been broadly used in many context such as in optical microscopy [9], medical imaging [10], hyper-spectral [11] and pancromatic imaging [12], anti-tank landmine detection [13], and many others applications.

Currently, image fusion allows merging images from multiple sensors or even multiple images from the same sensor [14][15][10]. Its goal is to integrate complementary information to provide a composite image which could be used to better understanding of the entire scene. A common found problem can be to fuse multifocus images, which are acquired from optical imaging systems. The challenge is to obtain a resulting fused image that contains enough-sharp information.

Generally, a current solution in multifocus image fusion is to reconstruct an image of the whole specimen by acquiring multi-focus images corresponding to each focused plane of the sample. The important thing is to find from each slice-image the region that is better focused in order to obtain an overall fused image with enough contrast in all the field of view. As we will see in this chapter, the digital image fusion methods take different in-focus parts of a sample and digitally or numerically combine them into a single composite image which contains the entire focused scene.

Many works have been published related with multifocus image fusion schemes. However, the main amount of these papers work with monocromatic input images to get a final fused image. Only a few of them have proposed the fusion of multifocus color images, and less common in the particular application of using microscopic samples [3][6][16].

In this chapter, we have proposed a new method of fusion of color images by pixels based on the Modulus of the Gradient Color planes (*MGC*) [17][18]. This algorithm requires the computation of the gradient for each image-channel from a *RGB* image. The procedure is fast and generate high sharply fusion images. The main application of our method is in the context of optical microscopy. The microscopic samples used in this chapter are metallic and biological with several textures and with irregular surfaces.

This chapter is organized as follows: in section 2, it is described the modulus of the gradient of color planes algorithm. This algorithm is the core of the method. Section 3 is used to explain the image fusion scheme step by step. Experiments and image acquisition are described in section 4. In the section 5, the fusion results including fused images are shown. Finally, in section 6 a discussion of the results and the conclusions of the method performance are included.

2. The Modulus of the Gradient of the Color Planes (MGC)

It is not unknown that in the RGB space, color vectors of Red, Green and Blue components are related to each pixel of a RGB image, which is commonly given by,

$$\mathbf{C}(x,y) = R(x,y)\hat{\imath} + G(x,y)\hat{\jmath} + B(x,y)\hat{k}, \tag{1}$$

where $R(x,y)$, $G(x,y)$, and $B(x,y)$ are the RGB space channels and $\hat{\imath}$, $\hat{\jmath}$, and $\hat{k}$ the unitary direction vectors.

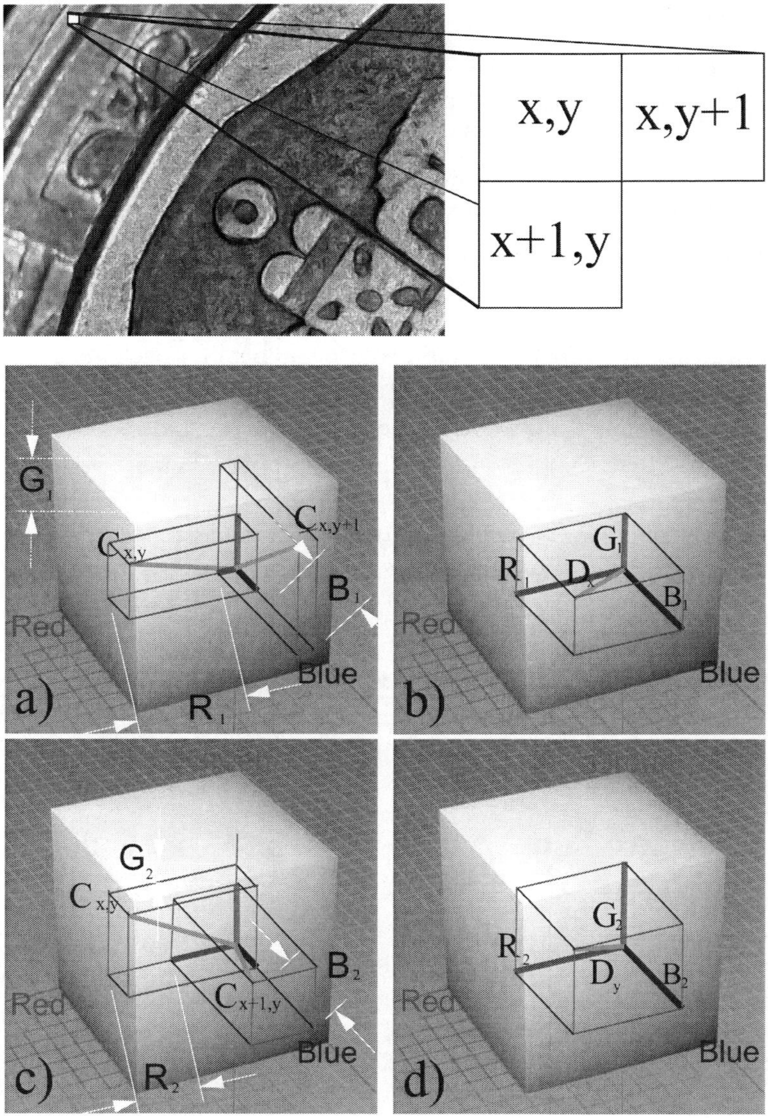

Figure 1. Modulus of the Gradient Color operator $|MGC[C(x, y)]|$ obtained by taking the Euclidean distance between color vectors.

A compound gradient image $I_C^g(x,y) = |MGC[C(x,y)]|$ can be reconstructed from the resulting images of the gradient modulus of $|\nabla R|$, $|\nabla G|$, and $|\nabla B|$. This compound image can be calculated by [19][20],

$$I_C^g(x,y) = \sqrt{\left(\frac{\partial R}{\partial x}\right)^2 + \left(\frac{\partial G}{\partial x}\right)^2 + \left(\frac{\partial B}{\partial x}\right)^2 + \left(\frac{\partial R}{\partial y}\right)^2 + \left(\frac{\partial G}{\partial y}\right)^2 + \left(\frac{\partial B}{\partial y}\right)^2}. \tag{2}$$

In general, the modulus of the gradient of the color planes I_C^g, is computed using the Euclidean distance as [18],

$$I_C^g(x,y) = |MGC[C(x,y)]| = \sqrt{\sum_{i=1}^{band}\left[\left(\frac{\partial C(x,y,i)}{\partial x}\right)^2 + \left(\frac{\partial C(x,y,i)}{\partial y}\right)^2\right]}, \tag{3}$$

where $i = 1, .., band$ is the dimensionality of the color space and $|MGC[C(x,y)]|$ is the color gradient operator. In the particular case of working with the RGB space, $band = 3$ is used. A vectorial sketch of computation of the modulus of the gradient color planes is shown in the Figures 1 and 2.

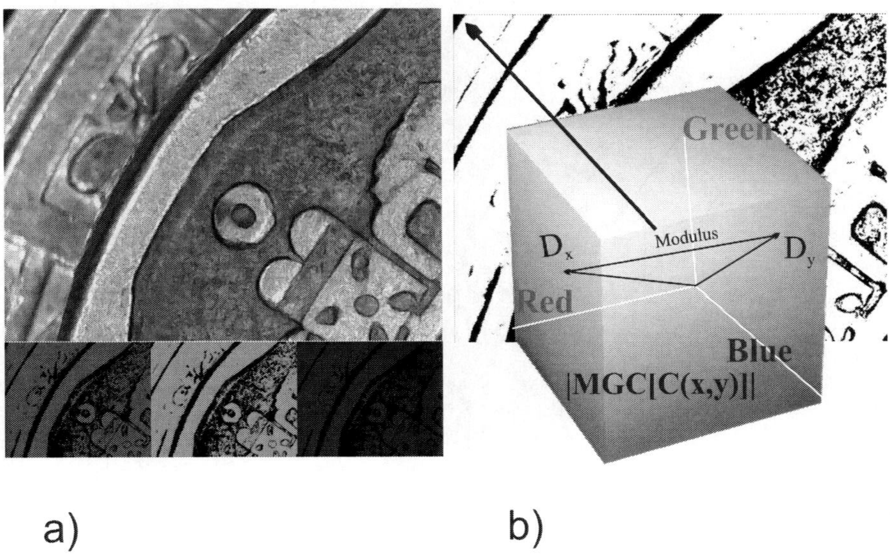

Figure 2. (a) Input color image and (b) MGC edge map.

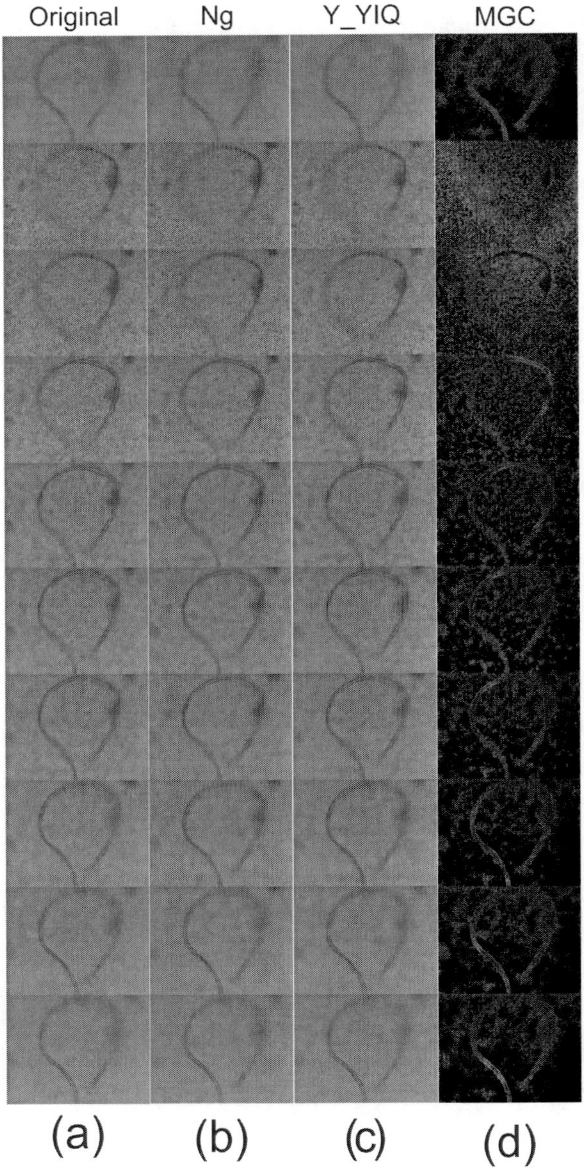

Figure 3. (a) Input color images, (b)intensity channel, (c) Y channel from the YIQ color space, and MGC edge map of (a).

Currently, the partial derivative along the $x - axis$ of a two-dimensional function $C(x, y, i)$ can be approximated by the difference,

$$\frac{\partial C(x,y,i)}{\partial x} \approx C(x,y,i) - C(x+1,y,i), \tag{4}$$

in a similar way, the partial derivative along the $y - axis$ is given by,

$$\frac{\partial C(x,y,i)}{\partial y} \approx C(x,y,i) - C(x,y+1,i). \tag{5}$$

Therefore, the modulus of the gradient color planes is an edge map that can be computed by the expression,

$$I_C^g(x,y) = \sqrt{\sum_{i=1}^{band} [(C(x,y,i) - C(x+1,y,i))^2 + (C(x,y,i) - C(x,y+1,i))^2]}. \tag{6}$$

In the Figure 3, the edges on an individual image directly in the color vector space are shown.

3. Image Fusion Scheme

Extended *DOF* in microscopy systems can increase the quantity of reachable most structural details available in thick specimens. Extended *DOF* have been obtained using different digital fusion methods. In this section, we propose a new approach to extended *DOF* through the modulus of the color gradient planes. We can start this section by establishing some definitions of the proposed method.

Let $C_j(x, y, i)$ be a $z - stack$ of N input color images, where $j = 1, .., N$. The index $i = 1, .., band$ represents the color channel. In order to highlight the details in the input images, we have used sharpening spatial filters known as Sobel H_k^S, Prewitt H_k^P, Kirsch H_k^K, and Frei-Chen $\frac{1}{2\sqrt{2}}H_k^F$. The four filters are shown in the Figure 4 and the mxn size in the Figure 5.

Therefore, a sharpening version $g_j(x, y, i)$ of the input color image $C_j(x, y, i)$ is reconstructed by the maximum pixel values from each k filtered image $C_j^k(x, y, i)$ as follows,

-1	0	1
-2	0	2
-1	0	1

H_0^s

-2	-1	0
-1	0	1
0	1	2

H_1^s

-1	-2	-1
0	0	0
1	2	1

H_2^s

0	-1	-2
1	0	-1
2	1	0

H_3^s

(a)

-1	0	1
-1	0	1
-1	0	1

H_0^p

-1	-1	0
-1	0	1
0	1	1

H_1^p

-1	-1	-1
0	0	0
1	1	1

H_2^p

0	-1	-1
1	0	-1
1	1	0

H_3^p

(b)

-3	-3	5
-3	0	5
-3	-3	5

H_0^k

-3	5	5
-3	0	5
-3	-3	-3

H_1^k

5	5	5
-3	0	-3
-3	-3	-3

H_2^k

5	5	-3
5	0	-3
-3	-3	-3

H_3^k

(c)

1	$\sqrt{2}$	1
0	0	0
-1	$-\sqrt{2}$	-1

H_0^F

0	1	$\sqrt{2}$
-1	0	1
$-\sqrt{2}$	-1	0

H_1^F

-1	0	1
$-\sqrt{2}$	0	$\sqrt{2}$
-1	0	1

H_2^F

$-\sqrt{2}$	-1	0
-1	0	1
0	1	$\sqrt{2}$

H_3^F

(d)

Figure 4. (a) Sobel, (b) Prewitt (c) Kirsch and (d) Frei-chen filters in the four cardinal directions.

$$F_j(x, y, i) = max_k[C_j^k(x, y, i)]. \tag{7}$$

Now, we can define a new fusion scheme Φ given by,

$$\Phi(x, y, i) = \begin{cases} C_1(x, y, i), & |MGC[F_1(x, y, i)]| \geq |MGC[F_2(x, y, i)]|, \\ C_2(x, y, i), & \text{otherwise.} \end{cases} \tag{8}$$

where $|MGC[F_j(x, y, i)]|$ is the modulus of the color gradient planes of $F_j(x, y, i)$ for $j = 1, 2$; which can be computed by Ec. (6). Schematically the image fusion procedure is shown in the Figure 6.

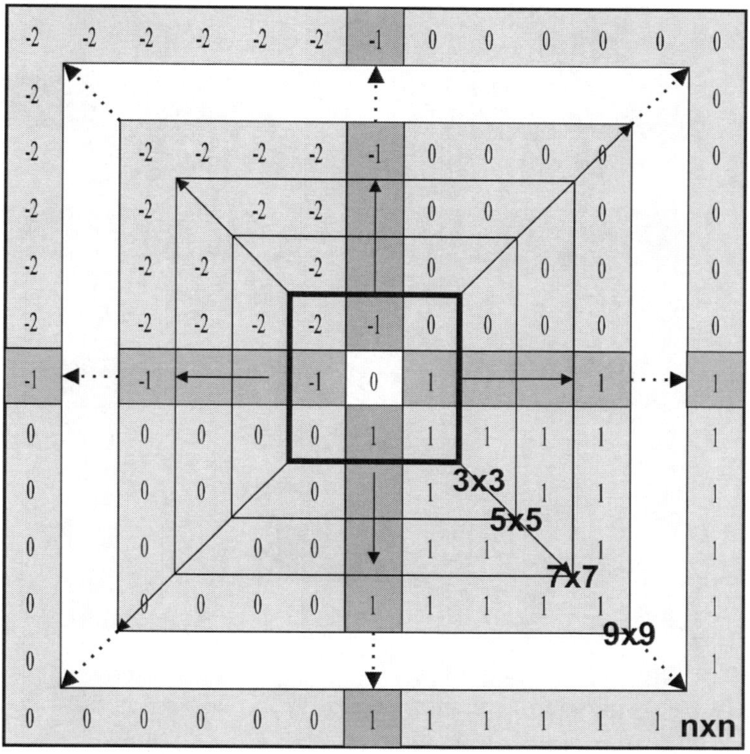

Figure 5. Sobel filters in the four cardinal directions for different sizes.

In order to measure the performance of the fusion algorithm, we have implemented the mean μ of the $\Phi(x, y, i)$ of the color fused image as follows,

$$\mu = \sum_{x=0}^{M-1} \sum_{y=0}^{N-1} MGC[\Phi(x, y, i)]. \tag{9}$$

This last value is related with the contrast of a color fused image.

4. Image Acquisition and Experiments

A motorized microscope Carl Zeiss Axio Imager $M1$ is used for the image acquisition of the biological test samples. This system contains an integrated

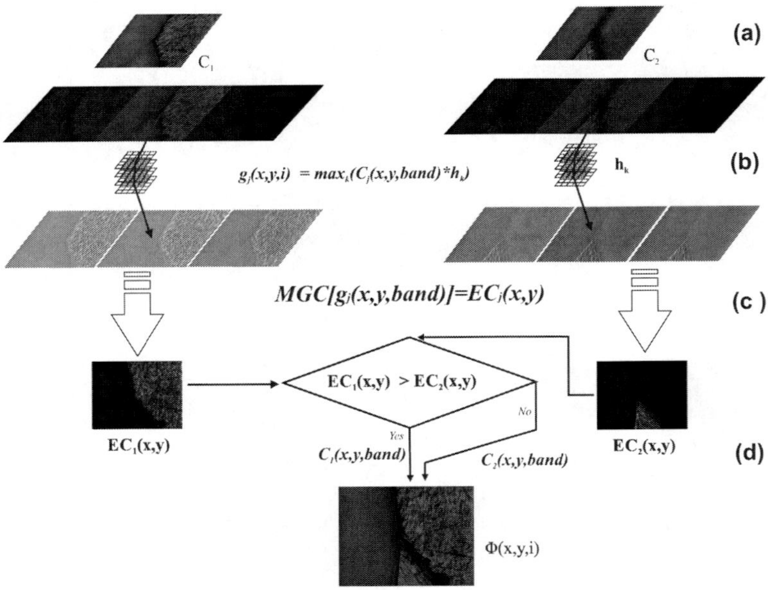

Figure 6. Steps of the fusion scheme. (a) input color images $C_j(x, y, i)$ where $j = 1, 2$, (b) sharpening version $g_j(x, y, i)$ of the input color images, (c) modulus of the color gradient operator of $g_j(x, y, i)$, (d) fusion rule based on the maximum pixel values from $|MGC[F_j(x, y, i)]|$.

AxioCam Mid Range Color camera of 5 megapixels with an image resolution of 2584 (H) X 1936 (V) pixels and a pixel size of $8.7mm$ X $6.6mm$. The microscope make uses of a $x - y$ platform where the sample is located and a motorized stage to control the $z - focus$ position is employed. The numerical aperture NA and the magnification M of the objectives of the microscope system used during the experiment are related according with the Table 1. This parameters will be used for the determination of the depth variation z.

The depth-of-focus $\Delta z'$ in the monochromatic case is defined as follows [21],

$$\Delta z' = \frac{n\lambda}{(NA)^2}, \tag{10}$$

where λ is the wavelength of the light and n the refractive index. The relation

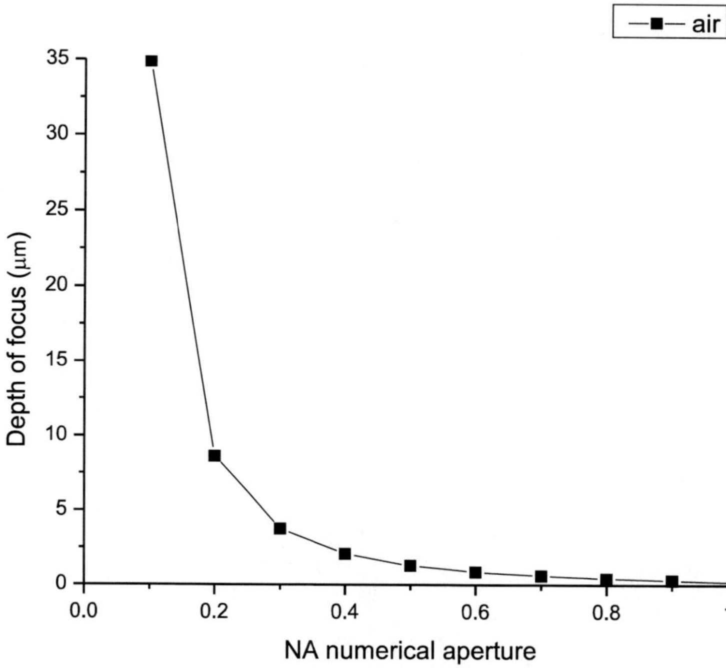

Figure 7. The depth-of-focus versus the *NA*.

Table 1.

Objective magnification	Numerical Aperture	Δz (*DOF*)
2.5X	0.16	50 micras
10X	0.30	20
40X	0.75	3
60X	0.9	2
100X	0.9	1

between depth-of-field Δz and depth-of-focus $\Delta z'$ is given by [21],

$$\Delta z' = M^2_{objective} \Delta z \frac{n'}{n}, \tag{11}$$

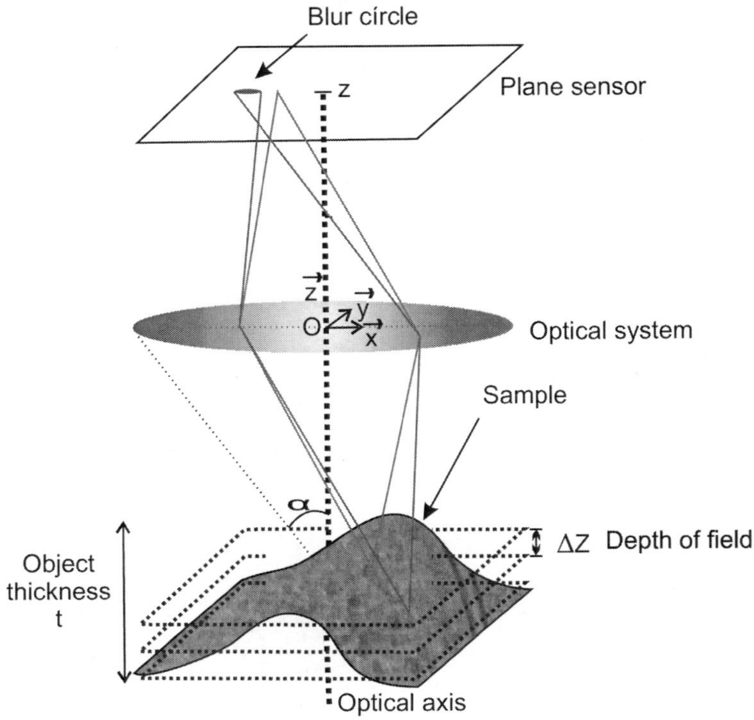

Figure 8. Microscopic imaging system.

where n' and n are, respectively, the media refractive indexes in the object and in the image space. The numerical aperture NA and magnification M are related by the following formula,

$$M = cteNA, \tag{12}$$

and

$$NA = nsin(\alpha). \tag{13}$$

where α is the angular semi-aperture on the objective side. As we can see, in Figure 7 when the numerical aperture is increased, the depth of focus becomes smaller. For the case of the *DOF*, it is sketched in the Figure 8.

In order to measure the effectiveness of our proposed algorithm, the Figure 9 shows a stack of slice-images of some real samples illuminated by means of the bright-field technique and at different z depth positions, with $z < \Delta z$.

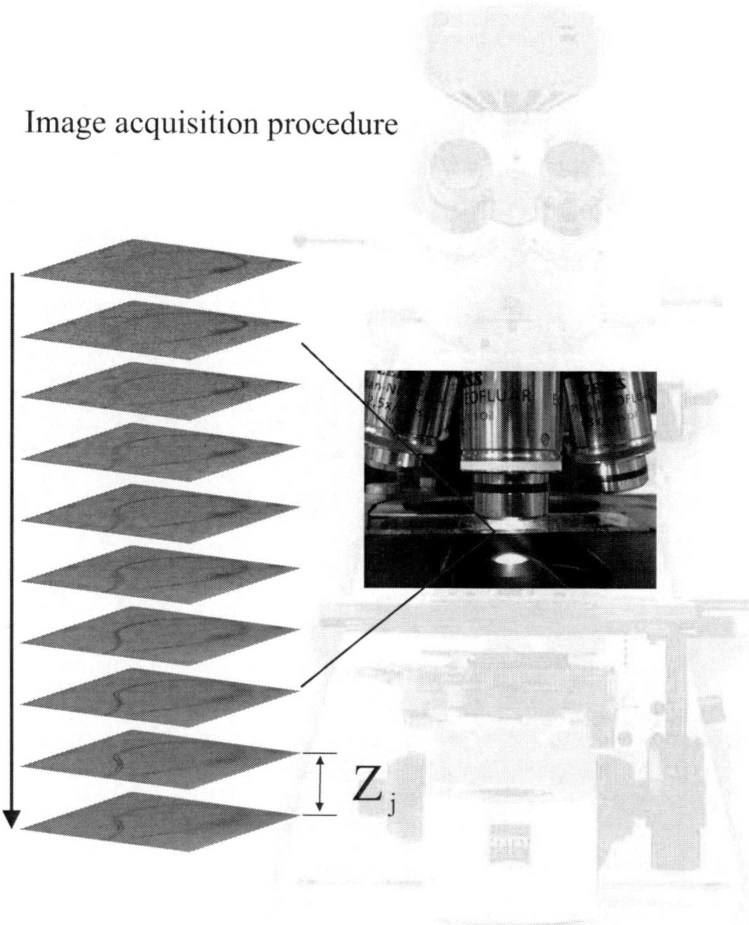

Figure 9. A $z-$stack of color slice-images from a biological sample which are acquired using the bright-field illumination technique at different $z-$depth positions.

5. Fusion Results

The digital color images which are taken from different focus planes of biological and metallic samples are shown in the Figures 10 and 11.

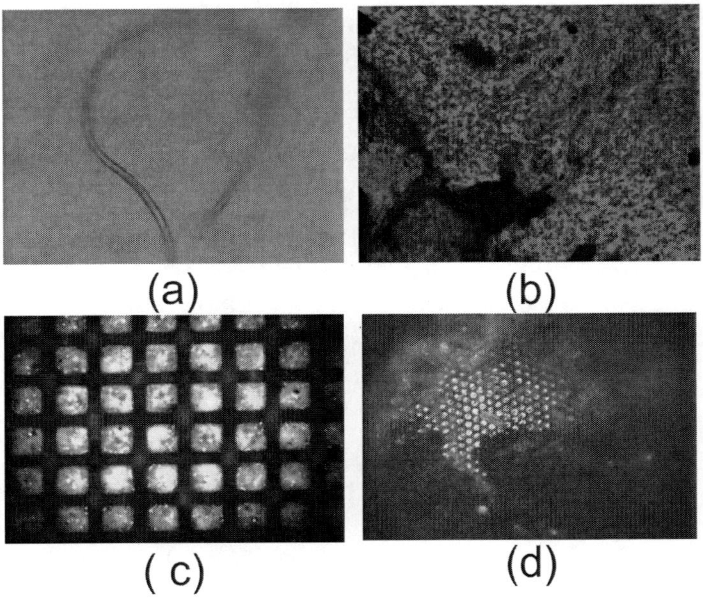

Figure 10. Test images acquired from biological samples of (a) bacillus of yogurt, (b) amniotic fluid, (c) tape to measure the glucose levels, and (d) bee eye. They are amplified by different objectives from amplifications of $10X$, $20X$, and $40X$ and $NA = 0.3, 0.5$, and 0.75 respectively.

In this part we analyze the effectiveness of using the fusion scheme implemented for multifocus color images. In our first case, the biological sample is a bacillus of yogurt. Digital images of a bacillus of yogurt are acquired at $M = 40X$, $N.A. = 0.75$, and an axial distance of $z = 3\mu m$ between the two focal planes. The fusion results using the enhancement MGC edge map with different sharpening filters are shown in the Figures 12 to 13.

In the second example, images of the same bacillus of yogurt are acquired but using the amplification $M = 10X$, and $N.A. = 0.3$. An axial distance of $z = 3\mu m$ between the three focal planes is considered. The fusion results using the enhancement MGC edge map with different sharpening filters are shown in the Figures 14 and 15.

In the third case the bacillus of yogurt is now acquired at $M = 20X$, $N.A. = 0.5$, and an axial distance of $z = 3\mu m$ between ten focal planes. The fusion results using the enhancement MGC edge map with different sharp-

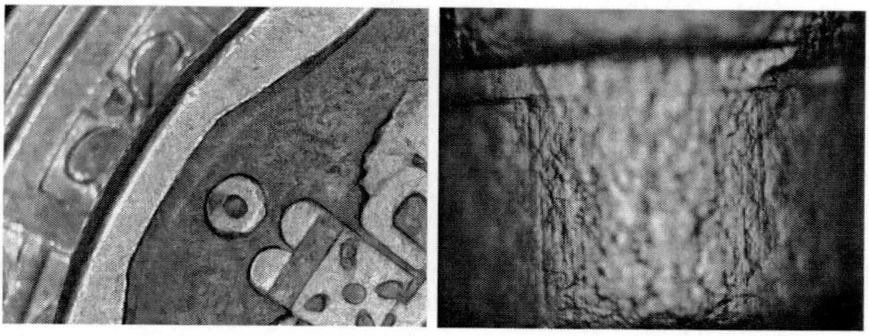

(a) (b)

Figure 11. Test images acquired from metallic samples. They are amplified by different objectives from amplifications of $10X$, $20X$, and $40X$. The numerical apertures are from $0.3, 0.5$, and 0.75 respectively. (a) coin, and (b) cylindric piece of metal.

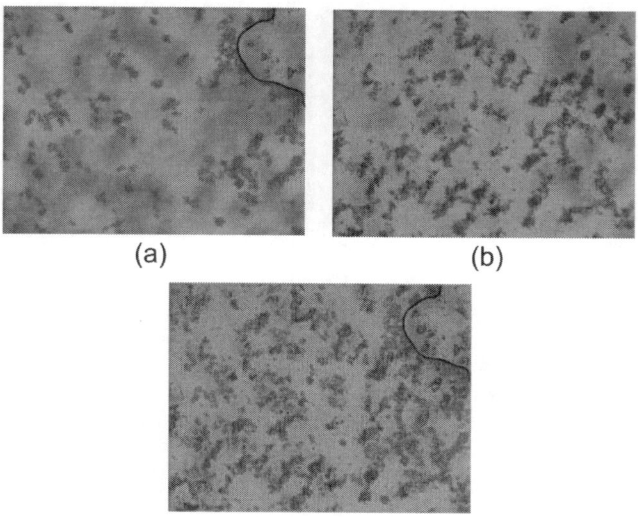

(a) (b) (c)

Figure 12. Bacillus of yogurt images acquired at $M = 40X$, $N.A. = 0.75$, and an axial distance of $z = 3\mu m$ between the two focal planes. (a) focal plane A, (b) focal plane B, and (c) Result of image fusion using the proposed enhancement MGC edge map.

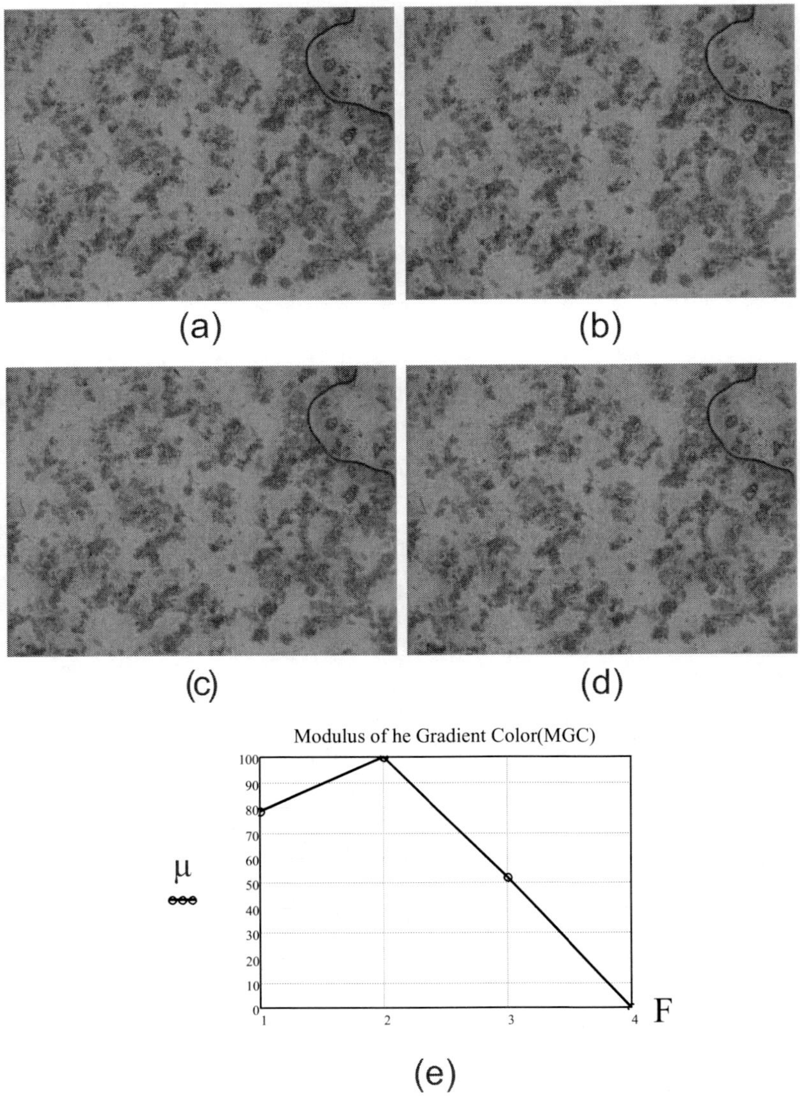

Figure 13. Results of image fusion using the proposed enhancement MGC edge map with the sharpening filters of (a) Frei-Chen (F=1), (b) Kirsch (F=2), (c) Prewitt (F=3), and (d) Sobel filter (F=4). (e) The results shown that the enhancement MGC edge map with Kirsch filter gives a major contrast fused image.

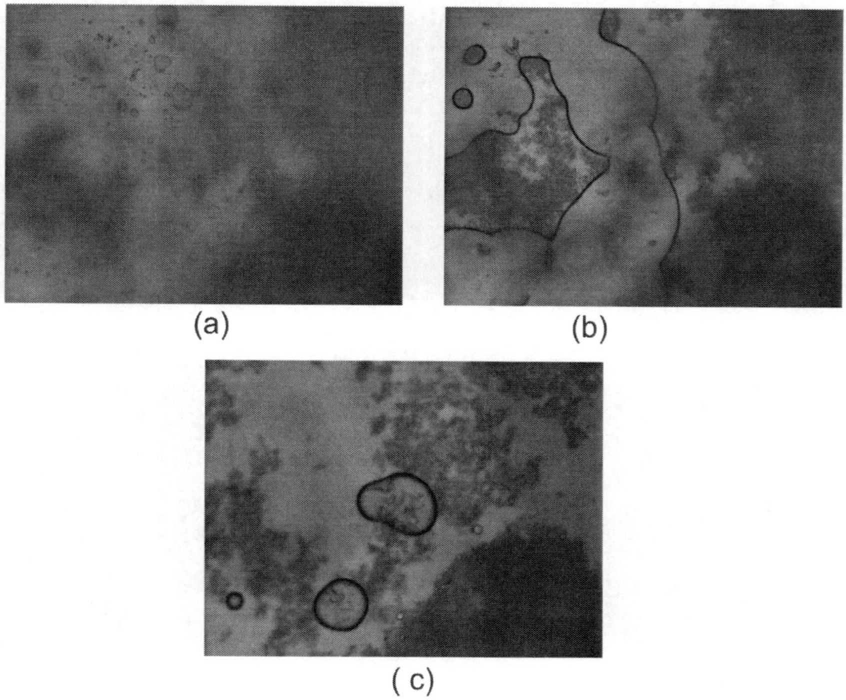

Figure 14. The sample is a bacillus of yogurt. The images are acquired at $M = 10X$, $N.A. = 0.3$, and an axial distance of $z = 3\mu m$ between the three focal planes. (a) focal plane A, (b) focal plane B, and (c) focal plane C.

ening filters are shown in the Figures 16 to 17. A major contrast fused image is obtained using the Kirsch filter.

An image of amniotic fluid is acquired at $M = 10X$, $N.A. = 0.3$, and an axial distance of $z = 10\mu m$ between the two focal planes. The fusion results using the enhancement MGC edge map with different sharpening filters are shown in the Figures 18 to 19. A major contrast fused image is obtained using the Kirsch filter.

An image of a tape to measure the glucose levels is acquired at $M = 10X$, $N.A. = 0.3$, and an axial distance of $z = 10\mu m$ between the two focal planes. The fusion results using the enhancement MGC edge map with different sharpening filters are shown in the Figures 20 to 21. A major contrast fused image is obtained using the Kirsch filter.

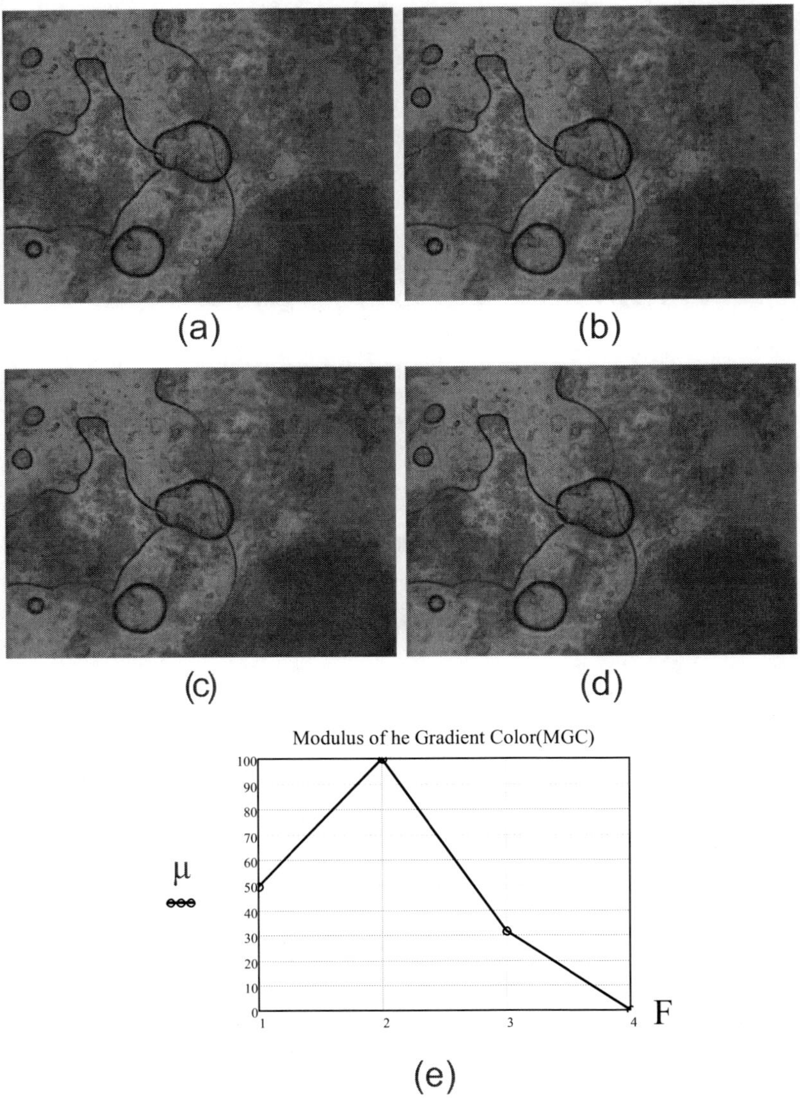

Figure 15. Results of image fusion using the proposed enhancement MGC edge map with the sharpening filters of (a) Frei-Chen (F=1), (b) Kirsch (F=2), (c) Prewitt (F=3), and (d) Sobel filter (F=4). The results shown that the enhancement MGC edge map with Kirsch filter gives a major contrast fused image.

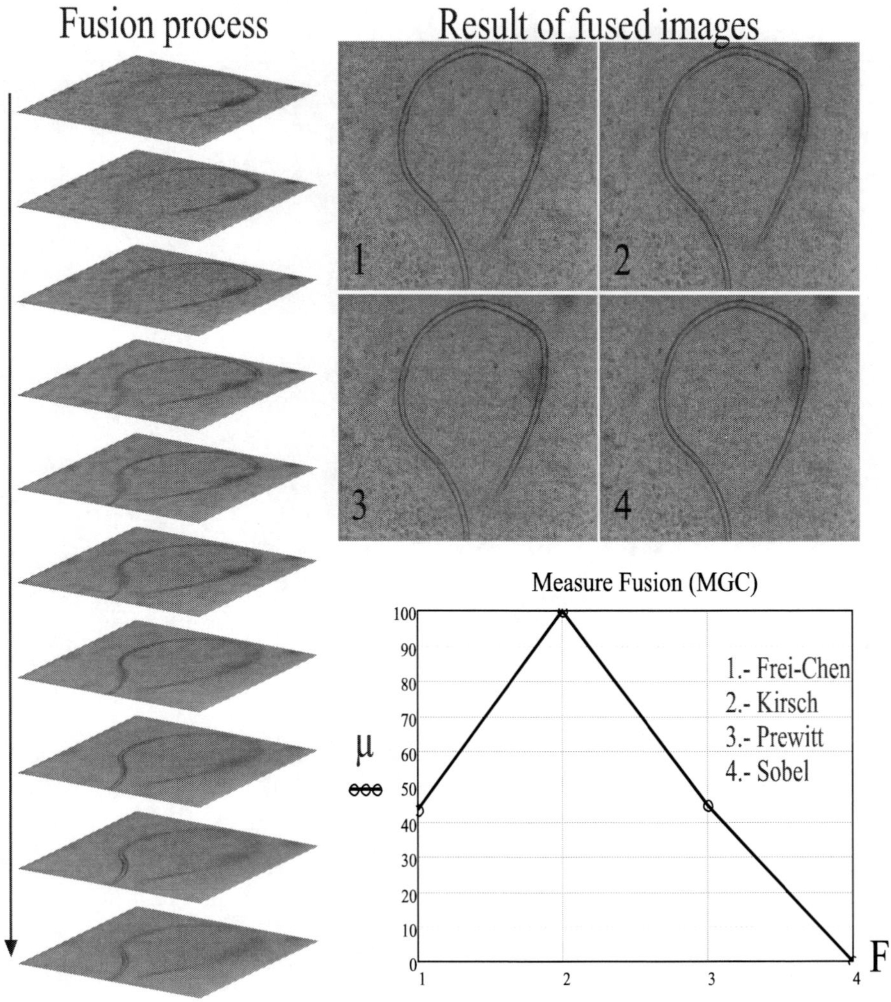

Figure 16. Results of image fusion using the proposed enhancement MGC edge map. The sample is a bacillus of yogurt acquired at $M = 20X$, $N.A. = 0.5$, and an axial distance of $z = 3\mu m$ between the ten focal planes. The results shown that the enhancement MGC edge map with Kirsch filter gives a major contrast fused image.

An image of bee eye is acquired at $M = 10X$, $N.A. = 0.3$, and an axial distance of $z = 10\mu m$ between the four focal planes. The fusion results using

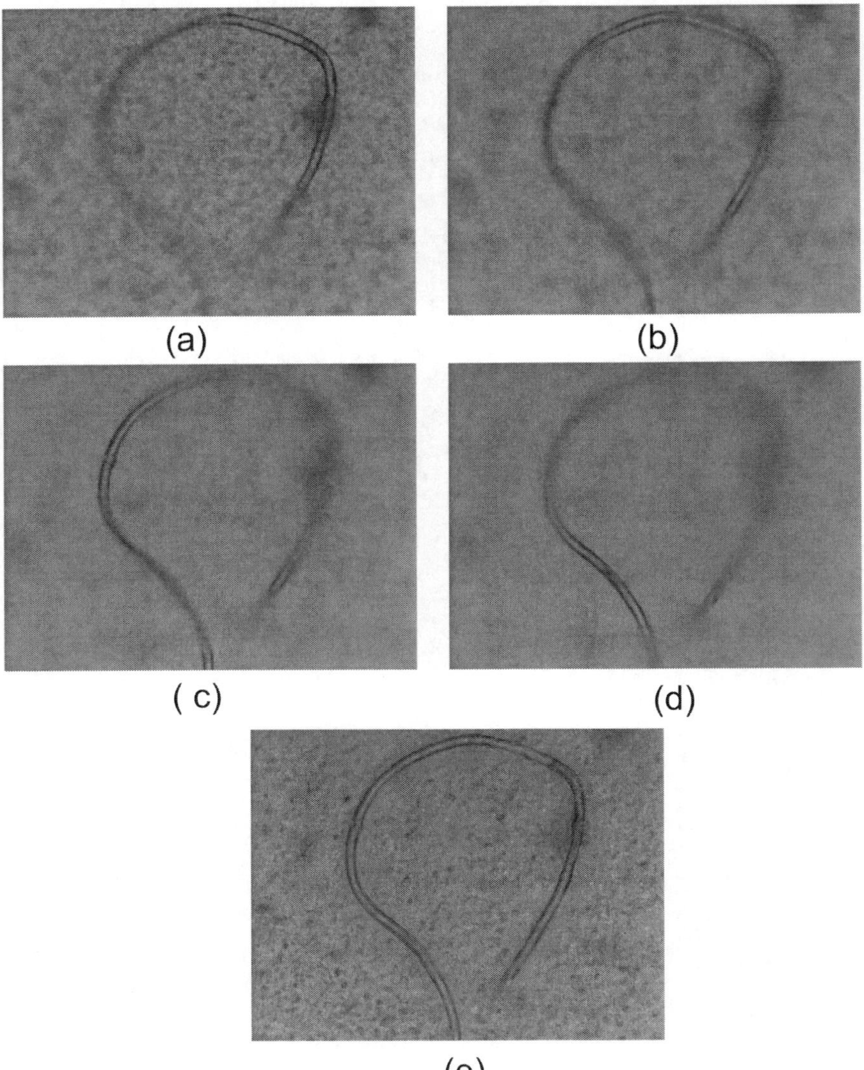

Figure 17. (a) focal plane 1, (b) focal plane 3, (c) focal plane 6 and (d) focal plane 9. Results of image fusion using the proposed enhancement MGC edge map with the sharpening Kirsch filter.

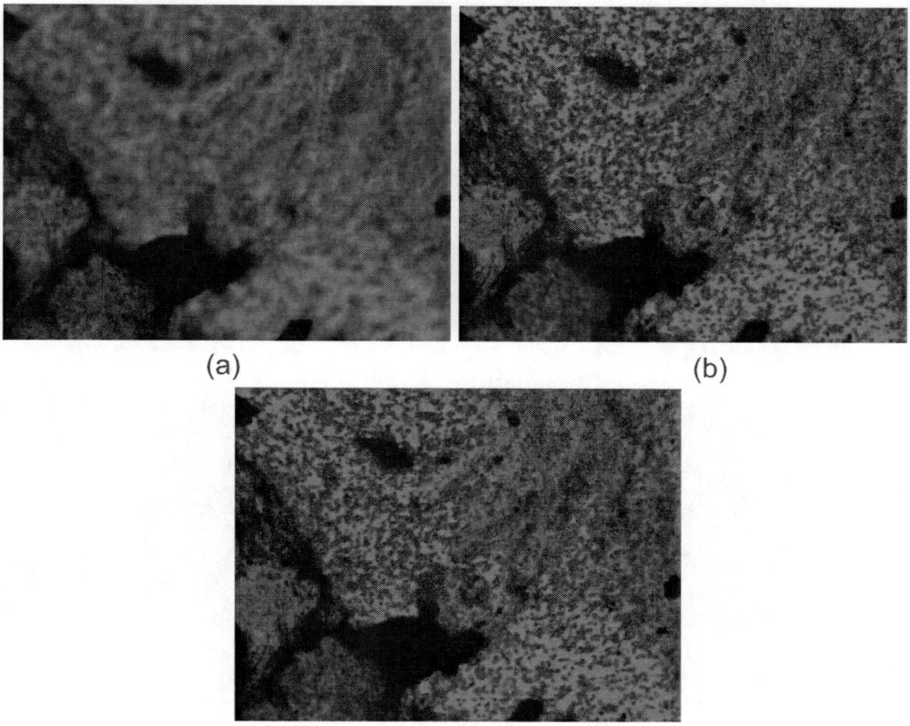

Figure 18. The sample is amniotic fluid. The images are acquired at $M = 10X$, $N.A. = 0.3$, and an axial distance of $z = 10\mu m$ between the two focal planes. (a) focal plane A, (b) focal plane B, and (c) fused image. The results shown that the enhancement *MGC* edge map with Kirsch filter gives a major contrast fused image.

the enhancement *MGC* edge map with different sharpening filters are shown in the Figures 22 and 23. Also a major contrast fused image is obtained using the Kirsch filter.

A stack-image of human tissue is acquired at $M = 2.5X$, $N.A. = 0.16$, and an axial distance of $z = 700\mu m$ between the four focal planes. The fusion results using the enhancement MGC edge map with different sharpening filters are shown in the Figures 24 and 25. A major contrast fused image is obtained using the Kirsch filter.

An image of a key is acquired at $M = 2.5X$, $N.A. = 0.16$, and an axial

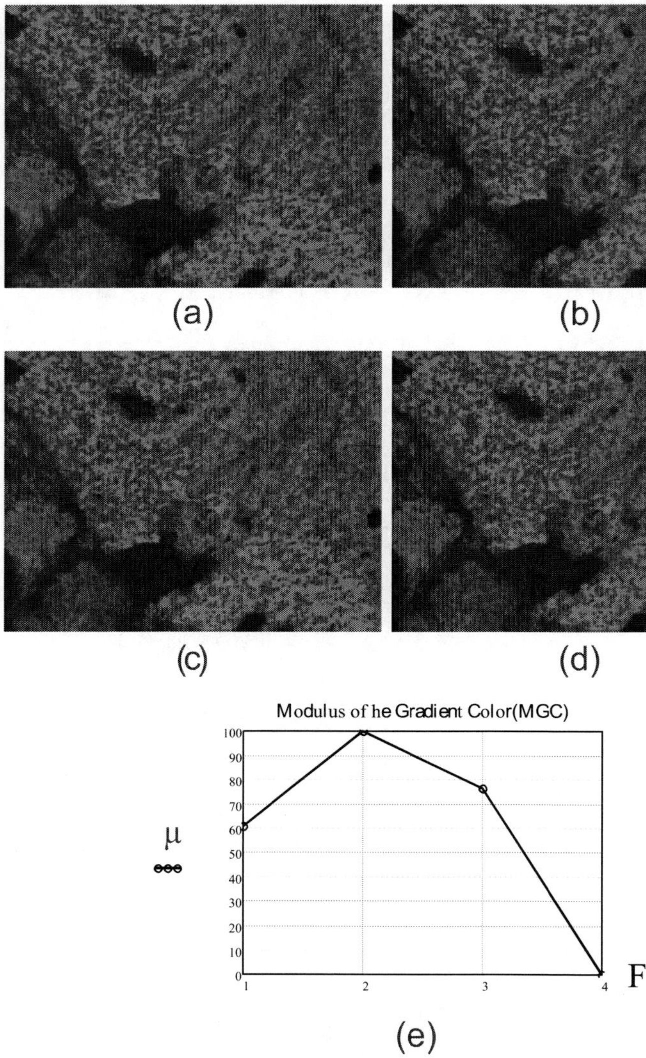

Figure 19. Results of image fusion by means of the proposed enhancement *MGC* edge map with the sharpening filters of (a) Frei-Chen (F=1), (b) Kirsch (F=2), (c) Prewitt (F=3), and (d) Sobel filter (F=4). The results show that the enhancement MGC edge map with Kirsch filter again gives a major contrast fused image.

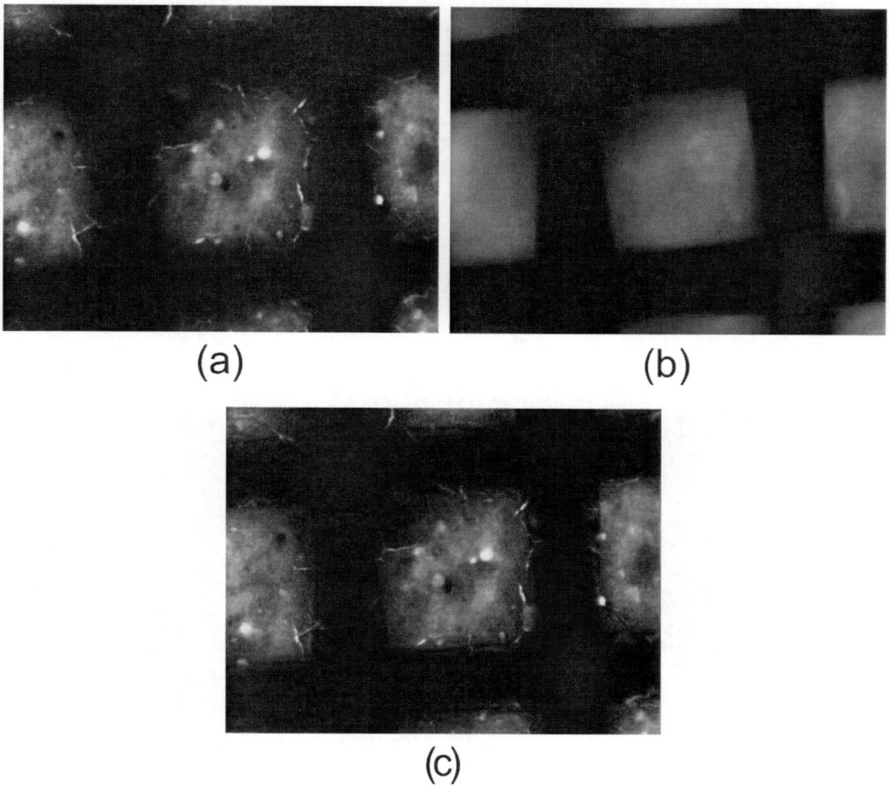

Figure 20. The sample is a tape to measure the glucose levels acquired at $M = 10X$, $N.A. = 0.3$, and an axial distance of $z = 10\mu m$ between the two focal planes. (a) focal plane A, (b) focal plane B, and (c) fused image. The results shown that the enhancement MGC edge map with Kirsch filter gives a major contrast fused image.

distance of $z = 2000\mu m$ between the two focal planes. The fusion results using the enhancement MGC edge map with different sharpening filters are shown in the Figures 26 to 27. A major contrast fused image is obtained using the Kirsch filter.

An image of a metallic key is acquired at $M = 2.5X$, $N.A. = 0.16$, and an axial distance of $z = 2000\mu m$ between the two focal planes. The fusion results using the enhancement MGC edge map with different sharpening filters

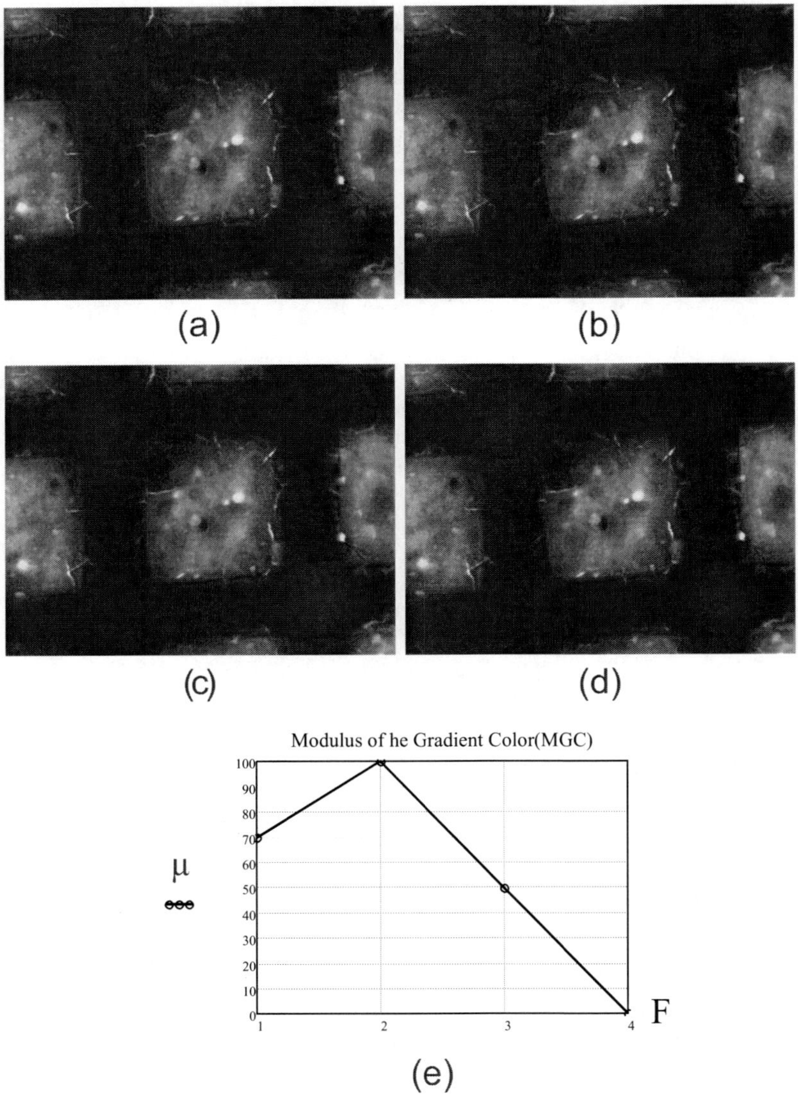

Figure 21. Results of image fusion using the proposed enhancement *MGC* edge map with the sharpening filters of (a) Frei-Chen (F=1), (b) Kirsch (F=2), (c) Prewitt (F=3), and (d) Sobel filter (F=4). The results shown that the enhancement *MGC* edge map with Kirsch filter gives a major contrast fused image.

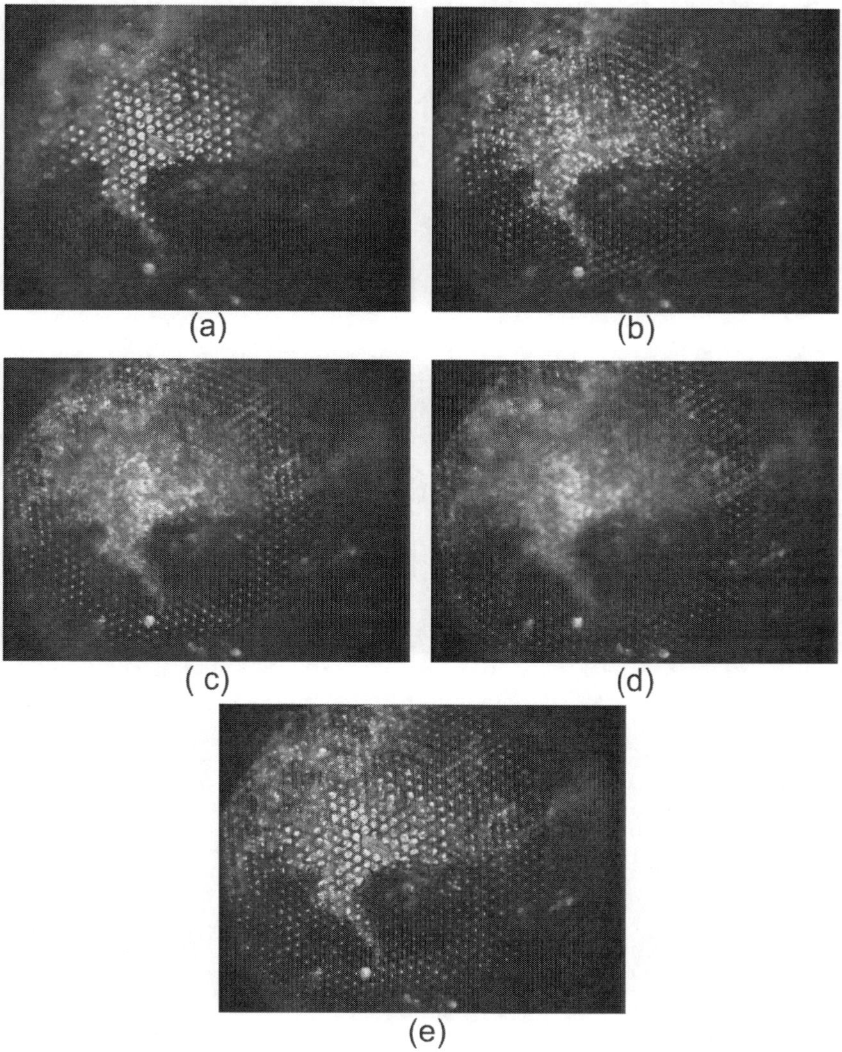

Figure 22. The sample is a bee eye acquired at $M = 10X$, $N.A. = 0.3$, and an axial distance of $z = 10\mu m$ between the four focal planes. (a) focal plane 1, (b) focal plane 2, and (c) focal plane 3, (d) focal plane 4, and (e) fused image. The results shown that the enhancement *MGC* edge map with Kirsch filter gives a major contrast fused image.

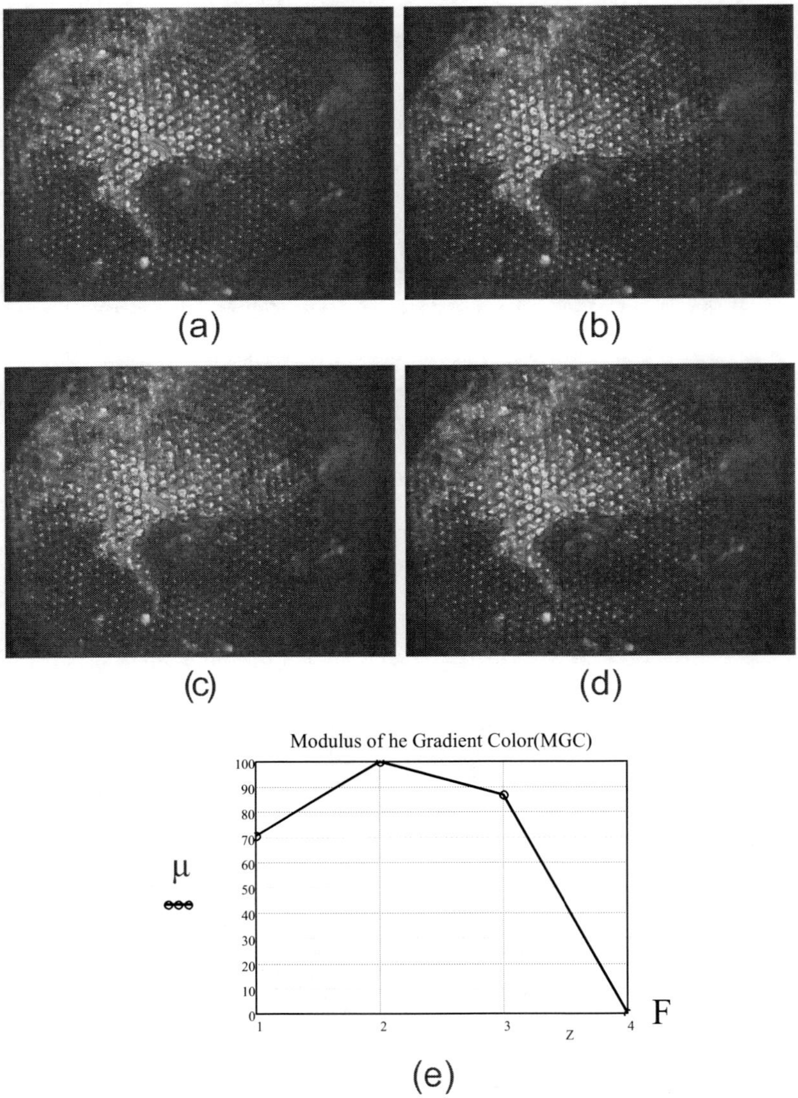

Figure 23. Results of image fusion using the proposed enhancement *MGC* edge map with the sharpening filters of (a) Frei-Chen (F=1), (b) Kirsch (F=2), (c) Prewitt (F=3), and (d) Sobel filter (F=4). The results shown that the enhancement *MGC* edge map with Kirsch filter gives a major contrast fused image.

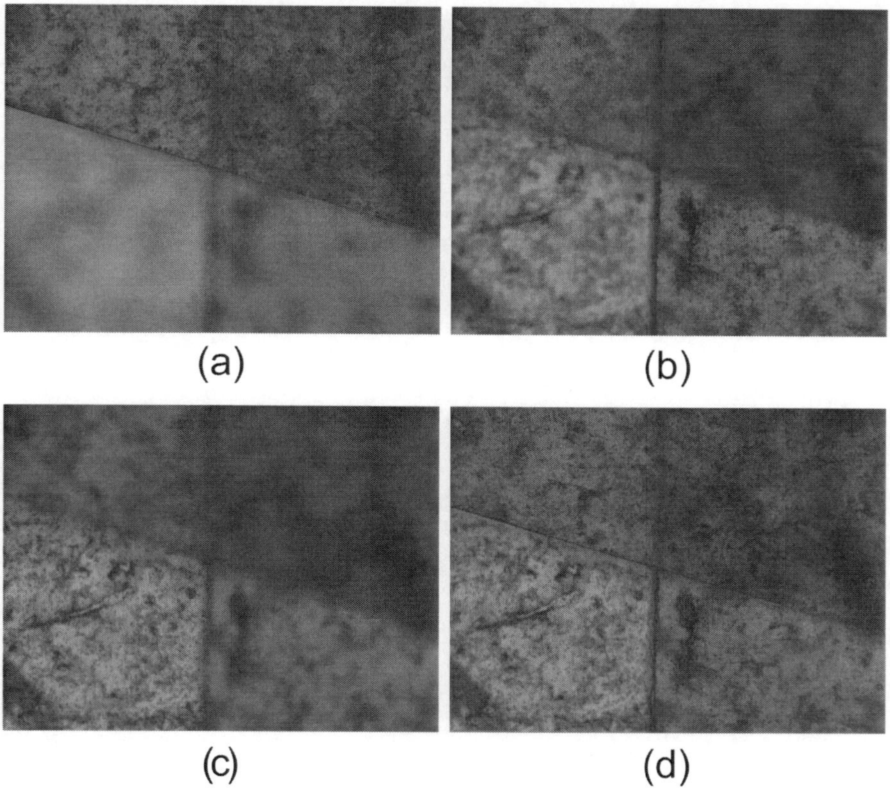

Figure 24. The sample is human tissue acquired at $M = 10X$, $N.A. = 0.3$, and an axial distance of $z = 10\mu m$ between the four focal planes. (a) focal plane 1, (b) focal plane 2, and (c) focal plane 3, (d) focal plane 4, and (e) fused image. The results show that the enhancement *MGC* edge map with Kirsch filter gives a major contrast fused image.

are shown in the Figures 26 to 27. A major contrast fused image is obtained using the Kirsch filter.

6. Discussion and Conclusion

We have presented a novel procedure to extend the *DOF* of a microscopic system. The main contribution of our method is to obtain fused color images with

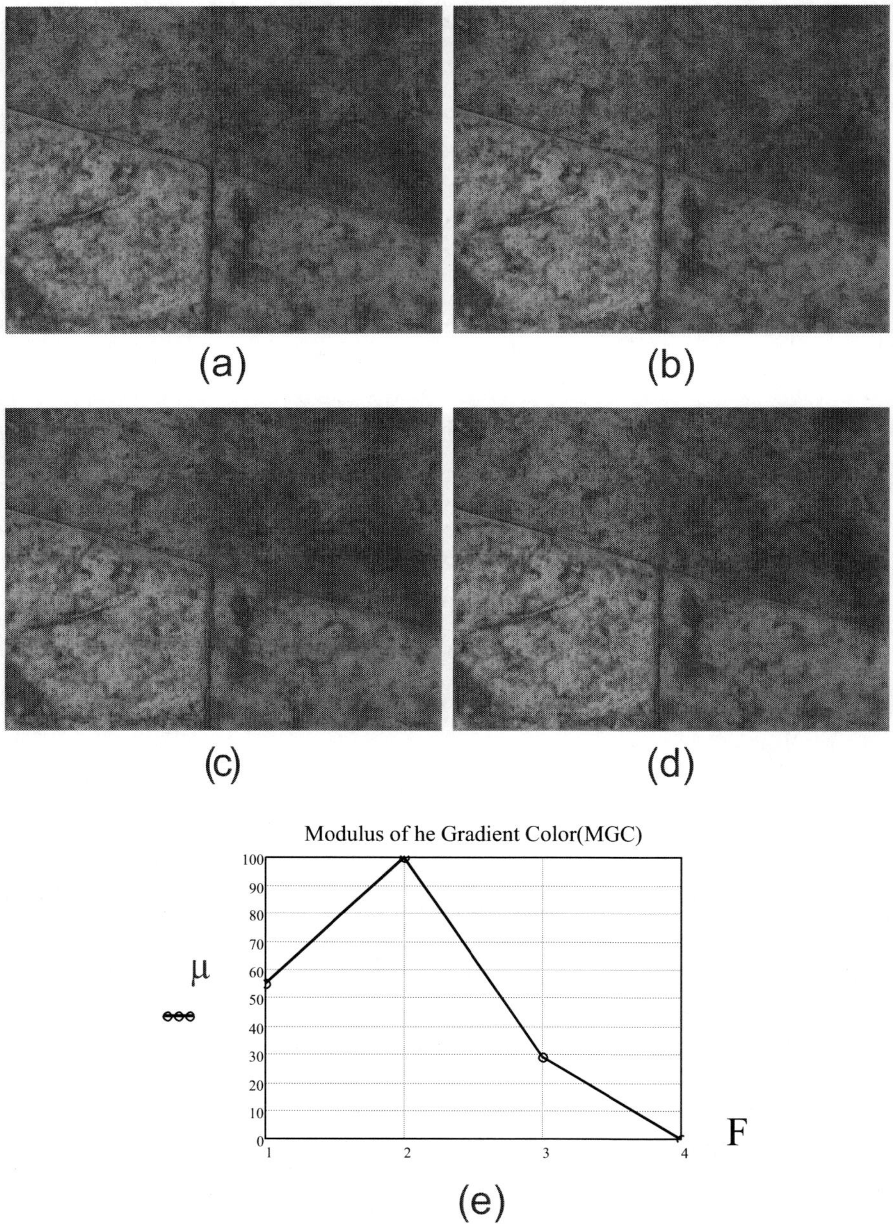

Figure 25. Results of image fusion using the proposed enhancement *MGC* edge map with the sharpening filters of (a) Frei-Chen (F=1), (b) Kirsch (F=2), (c) Prewitt (F=3), and (d) Sobel filter (F=4). The results show that the enhancement *MGC* edge map with Kirsch filter gives a major contrast fused image.

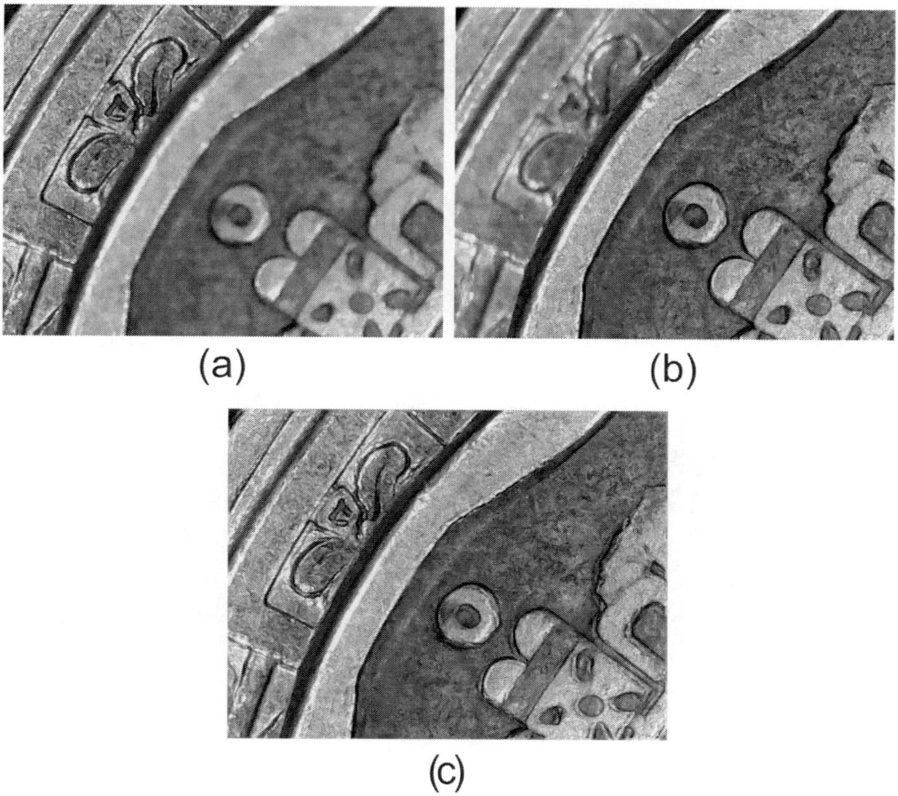

Figure 26. The sample is a metallic key. The image is acquired at $M = 2.5X$, $N.A. = 0.16$, and an axial distance of $z = 2000\mu m$ between the two focal planes. (a) focal plane 1, (b) focal plane 2, and (c) fused image. The results show that the enhancement *MGC* edge map with Kirsch filter gives a major contrast fused image.

high-frequency information from multi-focus color images.

We have proposed the Modulus of the Gradient of the Color planes MGC, which is commonly used as an edge detection method. The results shows that, the proposed enhancement *MGC* edge map can be implemented as a fusion scheme of multi-focus color images in the context of microscopy imaging.

Experimental results shows the effectiveness of the proposed method by testing several stacks illuminated with the bright-field technique. Images from

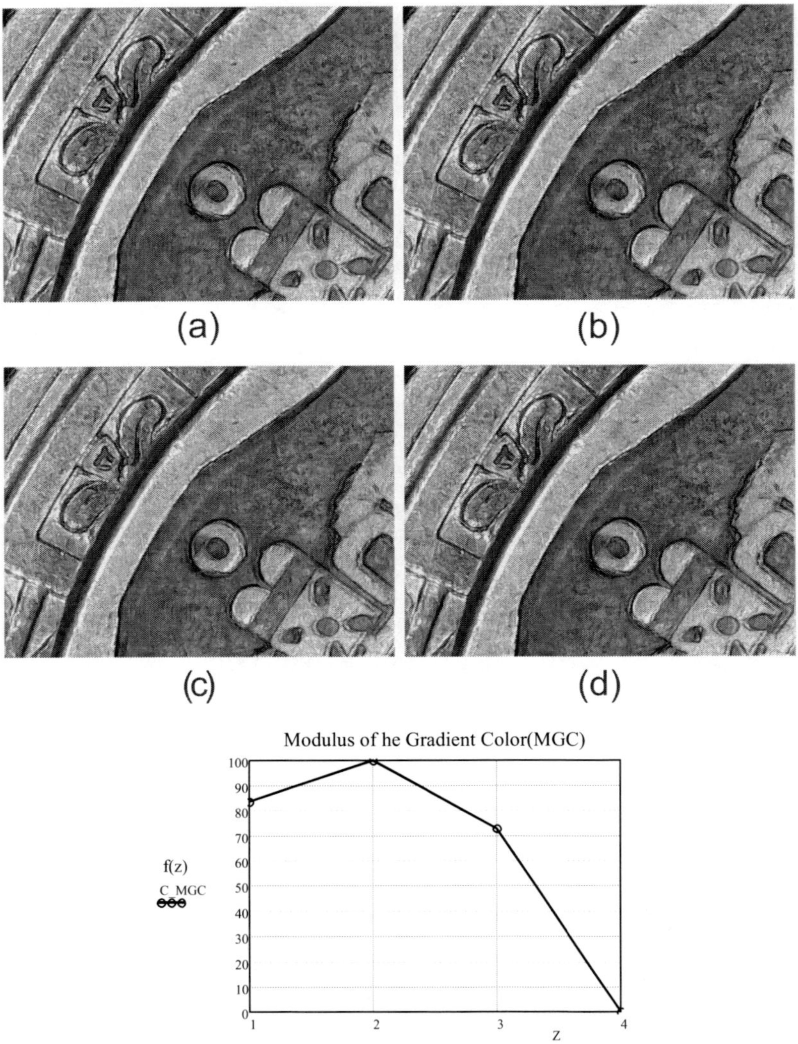

Figure 27. Results of image fusion using the proposed enhancement *MGC* edge map. Using the filters (a) Frei-Chen (F=1), (b) Kirsch (F=2), (c) Prewitt (F=3), and (d) Sobel filter (F=4). The results show that the enhancement *MGC* edge map with Kirsch filter gives a major contrast fused image.

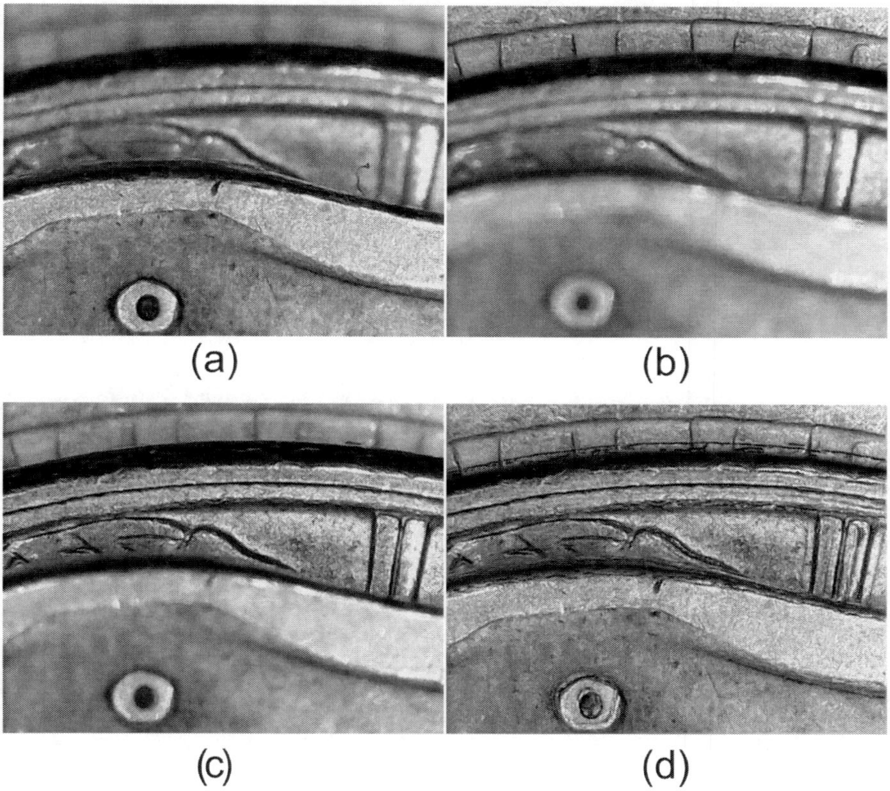

Figure 28. The sample is a key. The image is acquired at $M = 2.5X$, $N.A. = 0.16$, and an axial distance of $z = 2000\mu m$ between the three focal planes. (a) focal plane 1, (b) focal plane 2, (c) focal plane 2, and (d) fused image. The results show that the enhancement *MGC* edge map with Kirsch filter gives a major contrast fused image.

biological and metallic samples have been used to test the performance of the *MGC* algorithm. This *MGC* proposed algorithm is mathematically simple in comparison with other techniques as the wavelet transform. Also, the algorithm is fast to implement because it requires a small number of operations.

According with the qualitative and quantitative results, the final fused image contains the main details or the high frequency information of the multifocus input images. Also, the *MGC* edge map can be used as focus measure, it is

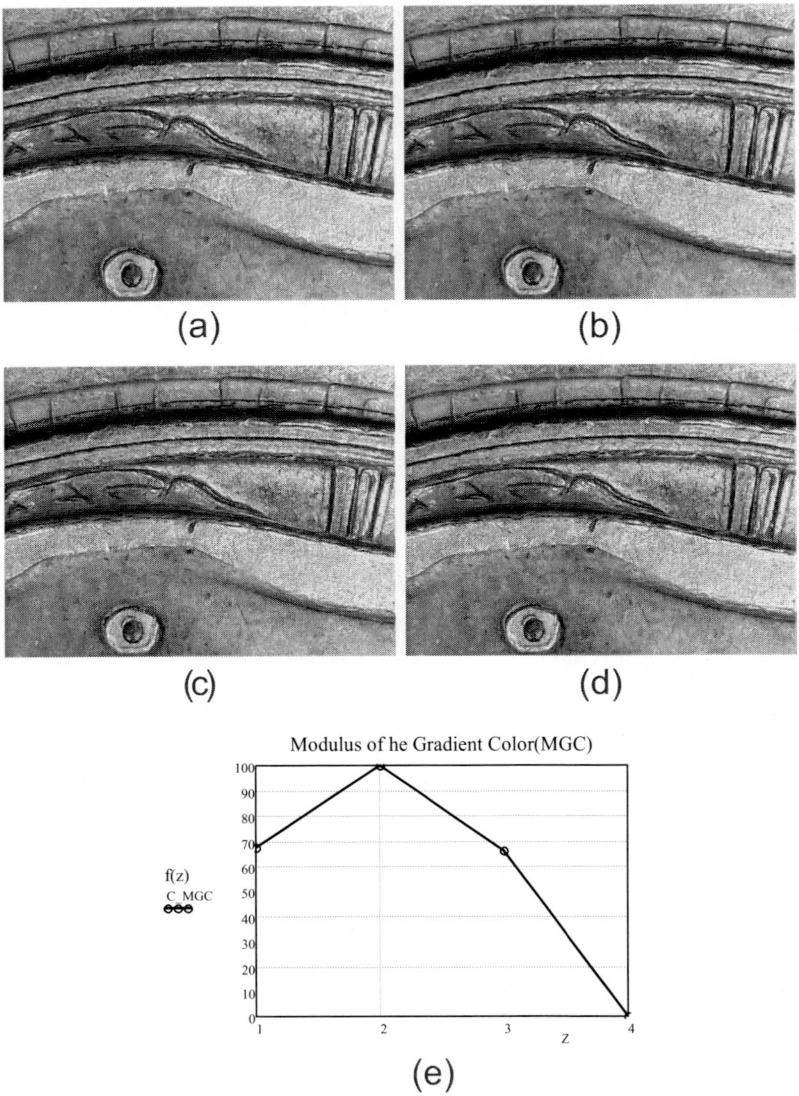

Figure 29. Results of image fusion using the proposed enhancement *MGC* edge map. Using the filters (a) Frei-Chen (F=1), (b) Kirsch (F=2), (c) Prewitt (F=3), and (d) Sobel filter (F=4). The results show that the enhancement *MGC* edge map with Kirsch filter gives a major contrast fused image.

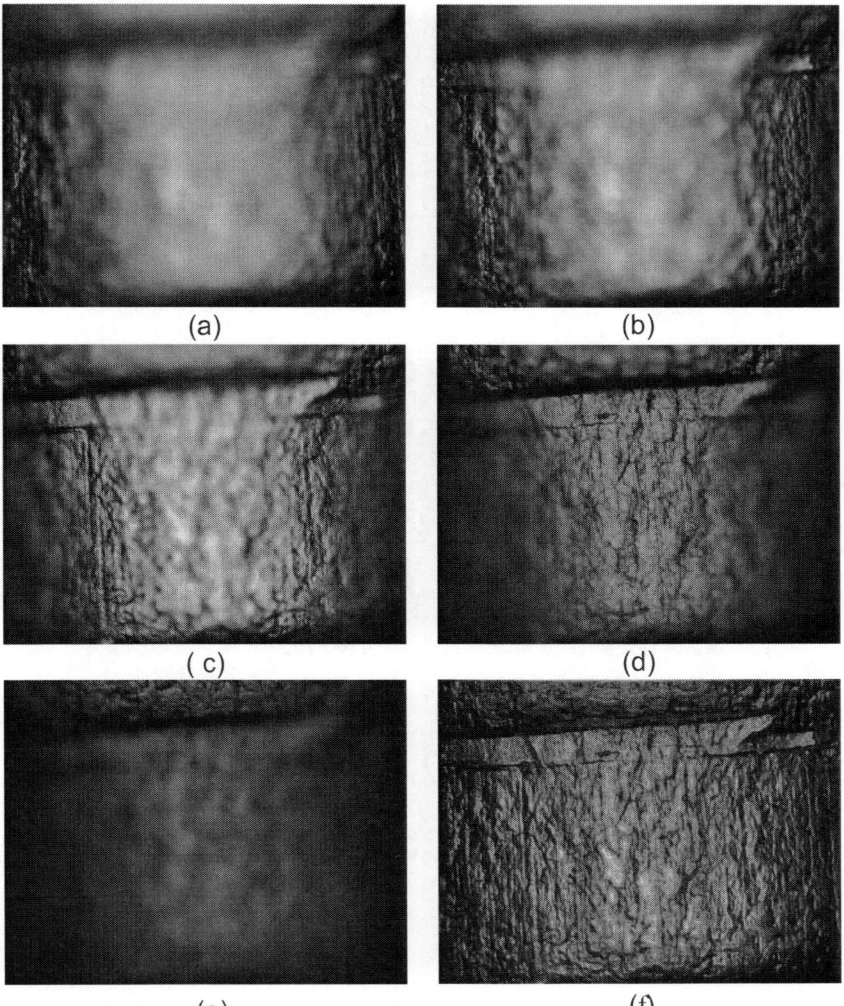

Figure 30. The sample is cylindric piece of metal. The image is acquired at $M = 20X$, $N.A. = 0.5$, and an axial distance of $z = 10\mu m$ between the sixteen focal planes. (a) focal plane 1, (b) focal plane 4, (c) focal plane 8, (d) focal plane 12, (e) focal plane 16, and (f) fused image. The results show that the enhancement *MGC* edge map with Kirsch filter gives a major contrast fused image.

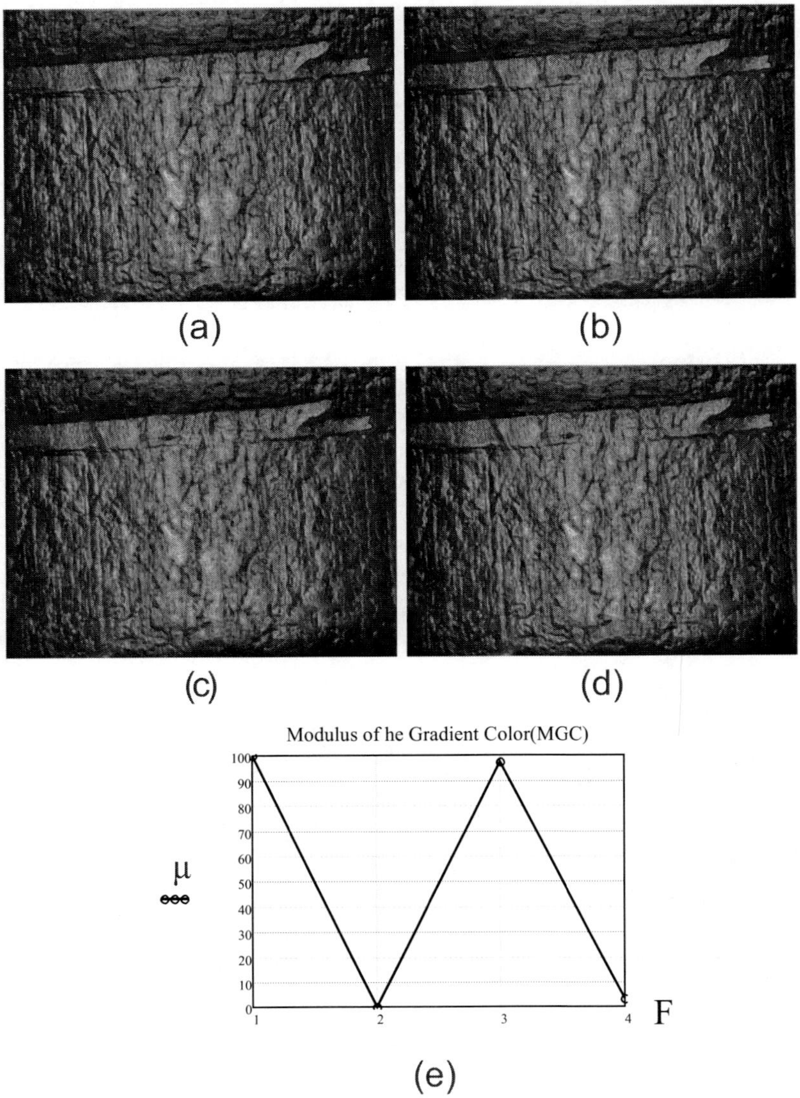

Figure 31. Results of image fusion using the proposed enhancement *MGC* edge map. Using the filters (a) Frei-Chen (F=1), (b) Kirsch (F=2), (c) Prewitt (F=3), and (d) Sobel filter (F=4). The results show that the enhancement *MGC* edge map with Frein-Chen and Kirsch filter gives a major contrast fused image.

also implemented for evaluating the contrast or sharpness of a color final fused image.

Minimum experimental conditions are required to acquire the digital images. Each fused image is obtained from a $z - stack$ of multi-focus images which are acquired at the same amplification and the same *NA*. If the magnification is constant in a specific image fusion using the *MGC* method then the overall fused image does not present artifacts. Additionaly, when illumination does not change along a $z - stack$ acquisition the fused image results do not present false color. The typical way to get constant illumination in the microscope is by means of a $kh\ddot{o}ler$ illumination system.

One of the important advantage of the proposed fusion method is that, it works for different amplifications of the samples. Practically, good results are obtained for all cases under study.

As preprocessing, we have used four different filters such as Frein-Chen, Kirsch, Sobel and Prewitt over the input images. The interest of taking into account these operations is to enhance input images before the *MGC* planes operator works. With this in mind, the *MGC* algorithm reach a better performance.

We can conclude that, *MGC* method preserves contrast of the input images, it does not generate visible artifacts in the fused image and it is easy-to-implement.

References

[1] E. R. Dowski and WT Cathey, "Extended depth of field through wavefront coding," *Applied optics*, 34 1859-1866 (1995).

[2] C. Toxqui-Quitl, Eva Acosta, Justo Arines, and A. Padilla-Vivanco, "Optimized restoration of wavefront coded images," *Proc. SPIE* 9192, Current Developments in Lens Design and Optical Engineering XV, 91921J (2014).

[3] S. Cheng et al., "An improved method of wavelet image fusion for extended depth-of-field microscope imaging," *Proceeding of the SPIE medical imaging*, 6144 (2006).

[4] C. Toxqui-Quitl, A. Padilla-Vivanco and G. Urcid-Serrano, "Multifocus image function using the Haar wavelet transform," *Proc. of SPIE* 6748, 555812-112 (2004).

[5] SA. Sugimoto, and Y. Ichioka, "Digital composition of images with increased depth of focus considering depth imformation," *Appl Opt* 24, 2076-2080 (1985).

[6] N. Goldsmith, "Deep focus: a digital image processing technique to produce improved focal depth in light microscopy," *Image Anal. Stereol* 19, 163-167 (2000).

[7] A. Padilla-Vivanco, I. Tellez-Arteaga, C. Toxqui-Quitl, and C. Santiago-Tepantlan, "Multifocus microscope color imagefusion based on Daub(2) and Daub(4) kernels of the Daubechies Wavelet family," *Proc. SPIE* 7443, (2009).

[8] J. Nuez, X. Otazu, O. Forse et al, "Multiresolution based image fusion with additive Wavelet decomposition," *IEEE Transactions Geoscience Remote Sensing* 37, 1204-12111 (1999).

[9] I.T. Young, et al., "Depth of focus in Microscopy," *Proc. of the 8th. Scandinavian Conference on Image Analysis*, 493-498, (1993).

[10] Guihong Qu, Dali Zhang, Pingfan Yan, "Medical Image Fusion by Wavelet Transform Modulus Maxima". *Optics Express* 4(9), 184-190(2001).

[11] Ketan Kotwal, Subhasis Chaudhuri, "A novel approach to quantitative evaluation of hyperspectral image fusion techniques," *Information Fusion* 14, 5-18, (2013).

[12] Shuyuan Yang, Min Wang, Licheng Jiao, " Fusion of multispectral and panchromatic images based on support value transform and adaptive principal component analysis," *Information Fusion* 13, 177-184 (2012).

[13] Hichem Frigui, Lijun Zhang, Paul Gader, Joseph N. Wilson, K.C. Ho, and Andres Mendez-Vazquez, "An evaluation of several fusion algorithms for anti-tank landmine detection and discrimination," *Information Fusion* 13, 161-174, (2012).

[14] Shutao Li, James T. Knok, Yaonan Wang, "Using the discrete wavelet frame transform to merge Landsat TM and SPOT panchromatic images," *Information Fusion* 3, 17-23(2002).

[15] G. Simone, A. Farina, F.C. Morabito, S.B. Serpico, L. Bruzzone, "Image fusion techniques for remote sensing applications," *Information Fusion* 4, 3-15(2002).

[16] Brigitte Foster, et al., "Complex wavelets for extended depth-of-field: A new method for the fusion of multichannel microscopy images ," *Microscopy reseach and technique* 65, 33-42 (2004).

[17] R. Hurtado-Perez, "Analisis comparativo de algoritmos de enfocamiento en imagenes a color para microscopia optica," *Tesis de Maestria*, Universidad Politecnica de Tulancingo, (2013).

[18] Theo Gevers, and Harro Stokman, "Classifying color edges in video into shadowgeometry, highlight, or material transitions," *IEEE transactions on multimedia*, 5(2), (2003).

[19] R. M. Rangayyan, B. Acha, and C. Serrano, "Color image processing with biomedical applications," *SPIE Press*, USA, (2011).

[20] Andreas Koschan and Mongi Abidi, "Digital color image processing," *Wiley interscience*, USA, (2008).

[21] Tomasz S. Tkaczyk, "Field guide to Microscopy," *SPIE Field Guides series*, USA (2009).

In: Image Fusion
Editor: C. T. Davis, pp. 83-119
ISBN: 978-1-63482-115-5

Chapter 4

FUSION AND CLASSIFICATION OF MULTISOURCE IMAGES FOR UPDATE OF FOREST GIS

D. Amarsaikhan* and N. Ganchuluun
Institute of Informatics and RS, Mongolian Academy of Sciences, Mongolia

Abstract

The main objectives of this chapter are to evaluate the performances of different image fusion techniques for the enhancement of spectral and textural variations of different forest types and toapply arefined maximum likelihood classifier for the extraction of forest class informationfrom the fused images in order to update a forest geographical information system (GIS). For the data fusion, modified intensity-hue-saturation (IHS) transformation, principal components analysis (PCA) method, Gram-Schmidt fusion, color normalization spectral sharpening, wavelet-based method, and Ehlers fusion are used and the results are compared. Of these methods, the better results are obtained through the use of the modifiedIHS transformation, PCA and wavelet-based fusion. The refined classification method uses spatial thresholds defined from contextual knowledge and different features obtained through a feature derivation process. The result of the refined classification is compared with the results of a standard method and it demonstrates a higher accuracy. Overall, the research indicates that multisource data fusion can significantly improve the interpretation and

* E-mail address: amar64@arvis.ac.mn (Corresponding author).

classification of forest types and the elaborated refined classification method is a powerful tool to increase classification accuracy.

Introduction

Forest is a very important natural resource that plays a significant role in keeping an environmental stability, ecological balance, environmental conservation, food security and sustainable development in both developed and developing countries[1]. In recent years, deforestation and forestland degradation have become the main concern for forest specialists and ecologists as well as policy and decision-makers dealing with the environment [2,3]. It has been found that much of the existing forests have been destroyed, mainly by shifting cultivation, timber preparation, legal and illegal logging, forest fires and increased number of people involved in agricultural activities [4,5,6,7]. To protect and conserve the deteriorating forest, it is vitally important for forest planners to have an updated forest map, integrate it with other thematic layers of a GIS and conduct sophisticated analysis.

In recent years, integrated approaches of optical and synthetic aperture radar (SAR) images have been increasingly used for forest mapping and analysis [8,9,10,11,12]. The combined application of optical and SAR data sets can provide unique information for different forest studies because passive sensor images will represent spectral variations of the top layer of the forest classes, whereas microwave data, with its penetrating capabilities, can provide some additional information about forest canopy. It is clear that the integrated use of the optical and microwave data sets can significantly improve forest class interpretation and analysis, because a specific forest type which is not seen on the passive sensor image may be observable on the microwave image and vice versa because of the complementary information provided by the two sources [13].

One of the prominent methods to combine remote sensing (RS) data from multiple sources is image fusion. Image fusion techniques usuallyattempt to combine images with different spectral and spatial resolutions and increase detailed information in the hybrid product produced by the fusion process [14,15,16]. Over the years, different fusion methods have been developed for improving spectral and spatial resolutionsof RS data sets. The techniques most encountered in the literature are the modified IHS transform, the Brovey transform, the PCA method, the Gram-Schmidt method, the local mean matching method, the local mean and variance matching method, the least square fusion method, the color normalization spectral sharpening, the wavelet-based fusion, the multiplicative method and the Ehlers fusion [17,18,19]. Most image fusion applications use modified approaches or combinations of these methods.

Traditionally, multispectral RS data sets have been extensively used for forest mapping and, for this purpose, diverse classification methods have been applied. The traditional methods mainly involved supervised and unsupervised methods and hence, a great number of techniques have been developed [20]. Unlike single-source optical data, data sets from multiple sources have proved to offer better potential for discriminating between different forest cover types. Many authors have assessed the potential of multisource images for the classification of different forest classes [21,22,23,24,25]. In RS applications, the most widely used multisource classification techniques are parametric methods, neural networks, decision tree classifier, Dempster–Shafer theory of evidence, and knowledge-based methods [26].

The aims of this chapter are(a) to investigate and evaluate different image fusion techniques for the enhancement of spectral and textural variations of different forest types, later to be used for training sample selection, and (b) to apply arefined maximum likelihood classifier for the extraction of forest class informationfrom the fused images in order to update a forest GIS. The selected fusion techniques are themodifiedIHS transformation, the PCA method, the Gram-Schmidt fusion, the color normalization spectral sharpening, the wavelet-based method, and the Ehlers fusion. For the refined classification, spatial thresholds defined from the contextual knowledge were applied. For the analysis, optical and SAR images with different spatial resolutions as well as some GIS data of the forest area in Mongolia wereused.

Study Area and Data Sources

As a test site, Bogdkhan Mountain situated in central part of Mongolia, near the Ulaanbaatar city has been selected. It is a strictly protected area and one of the world's oldest officially and continuously protected sites. Officially declared a sacred mountain reserve in 1778, evidence of its protected status dates back to the 13th century. Because of its universal natural or cultural significance, the mountain was added to the UNESCO World Heritage Tentative List on August 6, 1996 [27].Within the vicinity of this region, the cutting of trees, polluting rivers, hunting of wild animals or digging of the land are severely prohibited.

The mountain has a territory of 41651ha, of which 55% is covered by forest. The entire massif extends about 32km from the East to the West and 16 km from the North to the South. It has 588 species of high plants, which are related to 256 genuses of 70 families. The 135 species such as carex, artemisa, oxytropis that relate to 11 main genuses comprise 22.9% of all species distributed on the mountain. Forest is distributed on the altitude range of 1400m (1450m)- 2100m (2150m) above sea level and consists of 3 sub zones such as mountain plateau, taiga and taiga type. Cedar and larch dominate the forest cover but pine, birch, spruce and poplar also occur [8].

Figure 1. Landsat TM image of the Bogdkhan Mountain (R=band3, G=band4, B=band2). The size of the displayed area is about 28.2km x 20.0km.

The data used consisted of Landsat TM data from 31 July 2010 and Envisat SAR imageacquired on 25 March2010. The Landsat TM data have seven multispectral bands (B1: 0.45–0.52μm, B2: 0.52–0.60μm, B3: 0.63–0.69μm, B4: 0.76–0.90μm, B5: 1.55–1.75μm, B6: 10.40–12.50μm and B7: 2.08–2.35μm). The spatial resolution is 30 m for the reflective bands, while it is 120 m for the thermal band. In the current study, channels 2,3,4,5 and 7 have been used. The Envisat is a European Earth-observing satellite carrying a cloud-piercing, all-weather free polarimetric radar, which is designed to monitor the Earth from a distance of about 790km. In the present study, a C-band (i.e.5.36GHz) HH polarization image has been selected. In addition, a topographic map from 1969, scale 1:50,000 and a forest taxonomy map (made by the combined use of an aerial photograph from 1963 and ground survey from 1988), scale 1:100,000 were available, accordingly.

Figure 1 shows the study area in a Landsat TM image of 2010 and some examples of its forest cover.

Georeferencing of Multisource Images

In order to perform accurate data fusion, both high geometric accuracy and good geometric correlation between the images are needed. Initially, the Envisat image was rectified to the coordinates of the Landsat TMimage using 11 more regularly distributed ground control points (GCP)s defined from topographic and forest taxonomy maps of the study area. The GCPs have been selected on clearly delineated sites such as morphological structures, forest areas and roads. For the transformation, a second-order transformation and nearest-neighbour resampling approach were applied and the related root mean square (RMS) error was 0.526 pixels. The original and predicted coordinates as well as error values in both x and y directions are shown in Table 1. As seen from the Table 1, for each of the selected GCP, the RMS error is lower than 0.9 pixels. It indicates that there is a good geometric correspondence between the two images.

Table 1. The selected GCPs and total RMS error

No	Base X	Base Y	Warp X	Warp Y	Predict X	Predict Y	Error X	Error Y	RMS
1	4985.25	2652.75	2304.50	2068.50	2304.52	2068.51	0.021	0.011	0.0239
2	4046.00	1846.75	843.00	1151.00	842.82	1151.34	-0.174	0.349	0.3904
3	4070.50	1974.75	899.75	1320.25	899.43	1319.78	-0.313	-0.462	0.5584
4	4195.00	2472.25	1188.00	1978.00	1187.91	1977.95	-0.089	-0.041	0.0986
5	4660.00	1928.00	1704.00	1144.00	1704.02	1143.90	0.020	-0.091	0.0941
6	4535.25	2756.00	1706.00	2300.00	1705.99	2299.98	-0.007	-0.014	0.0168
7	4902.00	2348.00	2136.00	1669.00	2135.81	1668.88	-0.182	-0.115	0.2155
8	3888.00	2139.50	684.00	1584.00	684.20	1584.14	0.200	0.144	0.2474
9	4210.00	1790.50	1056.75	1042.00	1057.65	1041.27	0.900	-0.728	1.1582
10	4277.00	1799.00	1151.25	1038.75	1150.56	1039.45	-0.682	0.708	0.9840
11	4668.50	2288.75	1795.00	1630.75	1795.30	1630.98	0.302	0.235	0.3836

Total RMS Error: 0.526.

After the first co-registration of the coordinates, the combined Envisat SAR and Landsat TM images have been georeferenced to a UTM map projection using the topographic map of the study area. For the projection parameters, Zone 48N and WGS84 Datum were used. The GCPs have been selected on clearly delineated sites and, in total, 9 randomly distributed points were chosen. For the actual transformation, a second-order transformation was used. As a resampling technique, the nearest-neighbour resampling method was applied and the related RMS error was 0.35 pixels.

Speckle Suppression of the SAR Image and Derivation of the Texture Features

As the microwave images have a granular appearance, due to the speckle formed as a result of the coherent radiation used for radar systems, the reduction of the speckle is a very important step in further analysis. The analysis of the radar images must be based on the techniques that remove the speckle effects while considering the intrinsic texture of the image frame [28,29]. In this study, five different Speckle suppression techniques such as lee, local region, frost, kuan and gammamap filters [30] of 3x3 and 5x5 sizes were compared in terms of delineation of forested areas and texture information. After visual inspection of each image, it was found that the 3x3 gammamap filter created the best image in terms of delineation of different features as well as preserving content of texture information. In the output image, speckle noise was reduced with very low degradation of the textural information. Comparison of the selected and other SAR images is shown in figure 2.

In RS image analysis, texture is usually applicable to radar data. The ability to use radar data to detect texture and provide topographic information is a major advantage over other types of imagery [30]. To derive texture images, occurrence and co-occurrence measures (using 9x9 and 11x11 window sizes) were applied to the SAR image. The occurrence measures use the number of occurrences of each grey level within the processing window for the texture calculations, while the co-occurrence measures use a grey-tone spatial dependence matrix to calculate texture values [31]. By applying these measures, initially 20 features have been obtained, but after thorough checking of each individual feature, only 3features including the resultsof11x11 skewness, 9x9 contrast and 9x9 correlation filters were selected.

The skewness can be mathematically defined as the averaged cubed deviation from the mean divided by the standard deviation cubed. The contrast measure indicates how most elements do not lie on the main diagonal, whereas, the correlation measure is used to compare the similarity of two input signals as they are shifted by one another. The texture features can be used in several ways to increase the use of a SAR image. For example, adding the texturally enhanced radar image as an additional feature to the original data set should be useful for increasing the accuracy in a forest classification. Figure 3 shows the results of the skewness, contrast and correlation filters combined in a RGB (red, green and blue) domain.

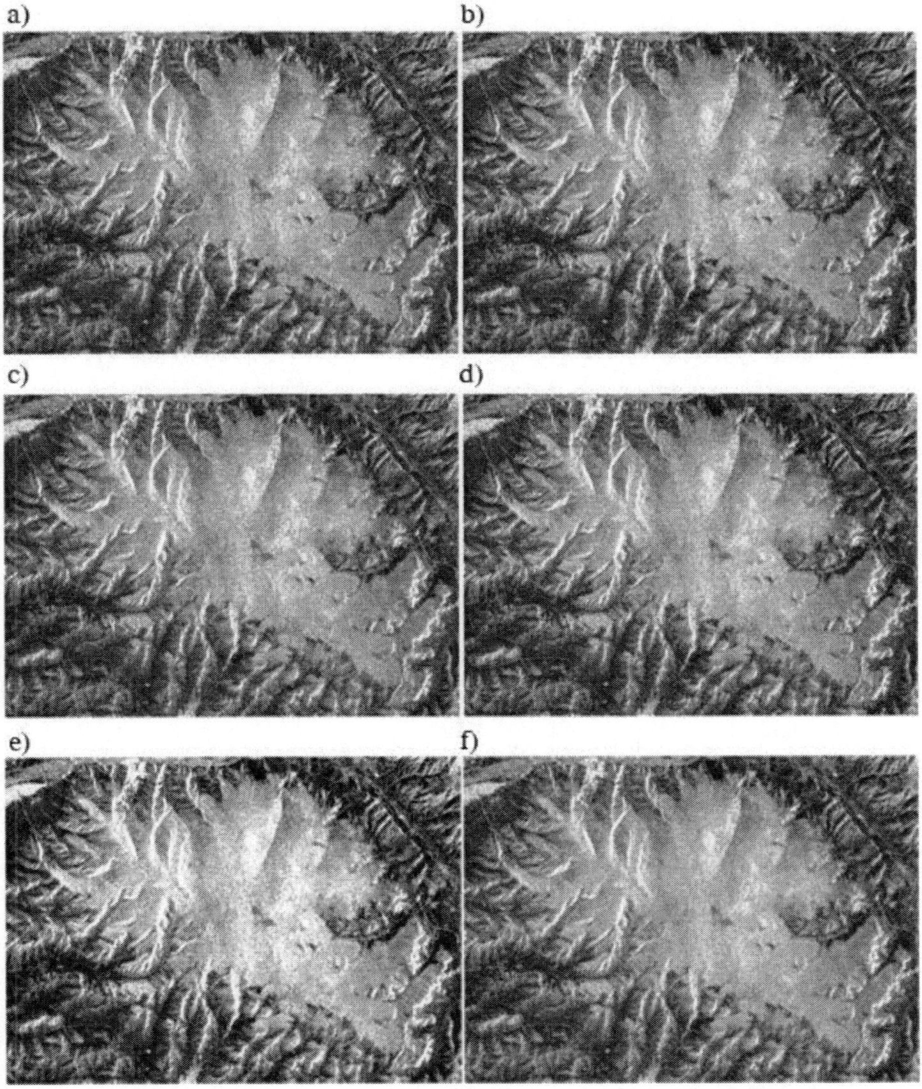

Figure 2. Comparison of the SAR images: (a) the original SAR image; (b) the image obtained by a 3x3 lee filter;(c) the image obtained by a 3x3 local region filter; (d) the image obtained by a 3x3 frost filter; (e) the image obtained by a 3x3 kuan filter; and (f) the image obtained by a 3x3 gammamap filter.

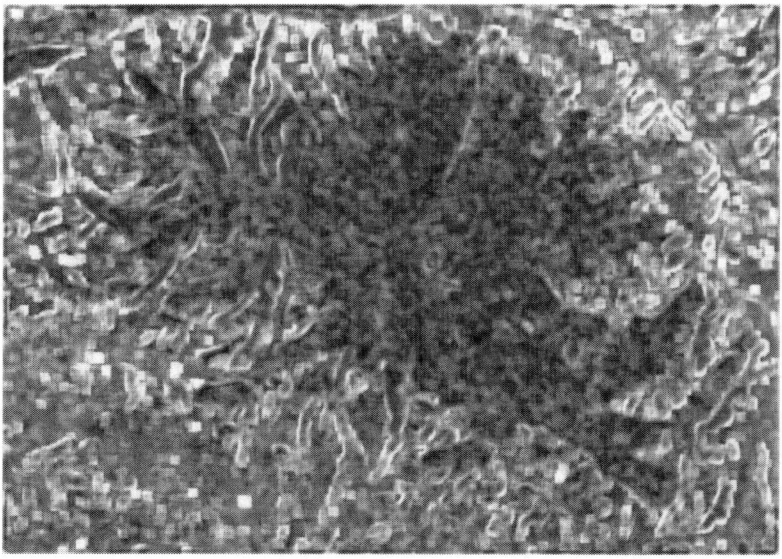

Figure 3. A colour image created by the texture filters (R=result of the contrast filter. G=result of the correlation filter, B=result of the skewness filter).

Image Fusion Methods

The image fusion refers to a process that integrates different images from different sources to obtain more information, considering a minimum loss or distortion of the original data. In other words, the image fusion is the integration of different digital images in order to create a new image and obtain more information than can be derived separately from any of them [16,32,33]. In the case of the present study, the SAR image provides some information about forest canopy due to radar's penetrating capabilities, while the TM image provides the information about the spectral variations of different forest classes. Over the years, different data fusion techniques have been developed and applied, individually and in combination, providing users and decision-makers with various levels of information. Generally, image fusion can be performed at four different stages: signal level, pixel level, feature level, and decision level [34]. In this study, data fusion has been performed at a pixel level and the following techniques were compared: (a) modifiedIHS transformation, (b) PCA method, (c) Gram-Schmidt fusion, (d) color normalization spectral sharpening, (e) wavelet-based method, (f) Ehlers fusion. Each of these techniques is briefly discussed below.

Modified IHS transformation: This method has a vast improvement over the traditional IHS for fusing satellite imagery; differing noticeably in spectral response. It allows combination of single-band panchromatic data with multispectral data, resulting in an output with both excellent detail and a realistic representation of original multispectral scene colors. In general, the HIS transformation separates spatial (intensity) and spectral (hue and saturation) information from a standard RGB image. The intensity refers to the total brightness of the image, hue to the dominant or average wavelength of the light contributing to the color and saturation to the purity of color. To fuse the images, three bands of a multichannel image are transformed from the RGB domain into the IHS color space. The panchromatic component is matched to the intensity of the IHS image and then replaces the intensity component. The modified IHS method is designed to produce an output that approximates the spectral characteristics of the input multispectral bands while preserving the spatial integrity of the panchromatic data. The technique works by assessing the spectral overlap between each multispectral band and the high resolution panchromatic band and weighting the merge based on these relative wavelengths [35].

PCA method: In RS image analysis, the PCA is usually considered as a data compression technique used to reduce the dimensionality of the multiband datasets [36]. It is also helpful for image encoding, enhancement, change detection and multitemporal dimensionality [32]. When the PCA is performed, the axes of the spectral space are rotated, changing the coordinates of each pixel in spectral space. The new axes are parallel to the axes of the ellipse. The length and direction of the widest transect of the ellipse are calculated using a matrix algebra. The transect, which corresponds to the major axis of the ellipse, is called the first principal component of the data. The direction of the first principal component is the first eigenvector, and its length is the first eigenvalue. A new axis of the spectral space is defined by this first principal component. The second principal component is the widest transect of the ellipse that is perpendicular to the first principal component. As such, the second principal component describes the largest amount of variance in the data that is not already described by the first principal component. In n dimensions, there are n principal components. Each successive principal component is the widest transect of the ellipse that is orthogonal to the previous components in the n-dimensional space and accounts for a decreasing amount of the variation in the data which is not already accounted for by previous principal components [30].

Gram-Schmidt fusion: This fusion technique transforms a set of multidimensional features into a new set of orthogonal and linear independent features. By averaging the multispectral bands, the method simulates a low resolution panchromatic band. As the next step, theGram-Schmidt transform is performed for the simulated panchromatic band and the multispectral bands with the simulated panchromatic band applied as the first band. Then the high spatial resolution panchromatic band replaces the first component [37]. Finally, an inverse transform is applied to create the spatially and spectrally enhanced multispectral bands.

Color normalization spectral sharpening: This is an extension of the color normalized algorithm. The input image bands are grouped into spectral segments defined by the spectral range of the panchromatic image. The corresponding band segments are processed in the manner that each input band is multiplied by the sharpening band and then normalized by dividing it by the sum of the input bands in the segment. Bands outside the spectral range of the panchromatic image are not sharpened [38]. Unlike many other sharpening techniques, this method can be used to simultaneously sharpen any number of bands and retain the input image's original data type and dynamic range.

Wavelet-based fusion: The wavelet transform decomposes the signal based on elementary functions, that is, the wavelets. By using this, an image is decomposed into a set of multi-resolution images with wavelet coefficients. For each level, the coefficients contain spatial differences between two successive resolution levels. In general, a wavelet-based image fusion can be performed either by replacing some wavelet coefficients of the low-resolution image with the corresponding coefficients of the high-resolution image or by adding high-resolution coefficients to the low-resolution data [39]. In the current study, the first approach, which is based on bi-orthogonal transforms, has been applied.

Ehlers fusion: This method is based on an IHS transform coupled with a Fourier domain filtering and it is extended to include more than 3 bands by using multiple IHS transforms until the number of bands is exhausted. A subsequent Fourier transform of the intensity component and the panchromatic image allows an adaptive filter design in the frequency domain. Using fast Fourier transform techniques, enhancement or suppression of the spatial components can be directly accessed. The intensity spectrum is filtered with a low pass filter whereas the panchromatic spectrum is filtered with an inverse high pass filter. After filtering, the images are transformed back into the spatial domain with an inverse fast Fourier transform and added together to form a fused intensity component with the low-frequency information from the low resolution multispectral image and the high-frequency information from the high resolution image. This new intensity component, the original hue, and the saturation components of the multispectral image form a new IHS image. As the last step, an inverse IHS transformation produces a fused RGB image. These steps can be repeated with successive 3-band selections until all bands are fused with the panchromatic band [40].

Interpretation and Comparison of the Fused Images

Initially, the aforementioned fusion techniques have been applied to the combined Landsat TM, Envisat SAR and texture images. In all cases, the SAR image was considered as a high resolution band. In order to obtain good colour images that can illustrate spectral and spatial variations of the available forest classes on the selected multisource image, all the fused images have been visually inspected and compared.

Table 2. Principal component coefficients from TM, SAR and texture images

Bands	PC1	PC2	PC3	PC4	PC5	PC6	PC7	PC8	PC9
TM2	0.091	-0.071	0.129	0.001	0.081	-0.001	-0.464	0.305	0.808
TM3	0.162	-0.12	0.222	-0.001	0.230	0.008	-0.675	0.263	-0.575
TM4	0.040	-0.038	0.100	0.023	-0.914	-0.001	-0.319	-0.218	-0.032
TM5	0.417	-0.285	0.576	0.025	-0.162	0.083	0.467	0.398	-0.030
TM7	0.282	-0.196	0.385	0.006	0.276	0.077	-0.081	-0.794	0.114
SAR	-0.799	-0.015	0.579	0.123	0.027	-0.097	0.010	0.001	-0.001
Contrast_F	-0.228	-0.915	-0.303	-0.109	-0.010	0.076	0.007	0.001	-0.001
Correlation_F	0.118	-0.107	0.002	-0.042	0.007	-0.985	0.0284	-0.027	0.001
Skewness_F	0.066	-0.095	-0.126	0.984	0.019	-0.024	-0.003	-0.001	-0.001
Eigenvalues	3392.8	2520.2	895.3	208.7	100.1	72.3	23.3	3.7	0.6
Variance (%)	47.00	34.92	12.40	2.89	1.38	1.00	0.32	0.08	0.01

In the case of the modifiedIHS transformation method, the fused image (Figure 4a) demonstrated a better result compared to some other combinations, because beside the improved textural enhancement, the image has good spectral separations among some coniferous and deciduous forests. However, on the image it was not easy to perceive the separations between spruce and cedar forests.

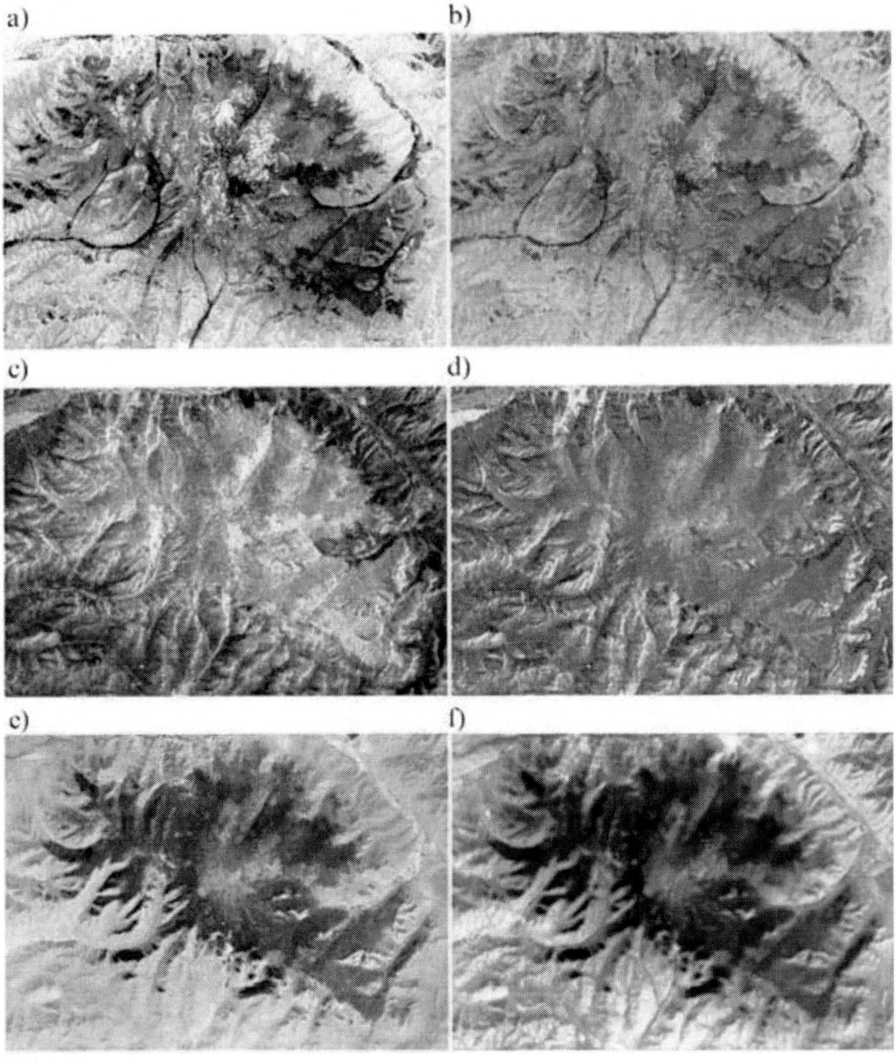

Figure 4. Comparison of the fused multisource images: (a) the image obtained by modified IHS transformation; (b) the PC image (red=PC1, green=PC3; blue=PC5); (c) the image obtained by Gram-Schmidt fusion; (d) the image obtained bycolor normalization spectral sharpening; (e)the image obtained by wavelet-based method; and(f) the image obtained by Elhers fusion.

PCA has been applied to all selected images and the result of the final analysis is shown in table 2. As can be seen from table 2, the Envisat HH polarisation image has a high negative loading in PC1 which contains 47% of the overall variance. This means that the PC1 is dominated by the characteristics of the SAR image. Although, PC2 contained 34.92% of the overall variance and had a very high negative loading of the result of the contrast filter, visual inspection revealed that it contained less information related to the available forest classes. In PC3 that contains 12.4% of the overall variance, the middle infrared band of TM and SAR image have moderately high loadings. Compared to the PC2, on this image, it was possible to see some tonal variations of different forest classes. It was seen that the PC4 dominated by the result of theskewness filter had no useful information. However, visual inspection of PC5 that contained only 1.38 % of the overall variance, in which near infrared band of TM had a very high negative loading, revealed that this feature contained useful information related to the tonal variations as well as textural characteristics of different forest classes. The PC6 and PC7 dominated by the negative characteristics of thecorrelation filter and visible bands had some useful information. The inspection of the remaining PCs indicated that they contained noise from the total data set. The PC image created by the combinations of PC1, PC3 and PC5 is shown in figure 4b. As seen from the PC image, though the image cannot show clear textural features, it could well illustrate the colour variations of different classes, specifically among larch, cedar, birch and spruce forests.

In the cases of the Gram-Schmidt fusion and color normalization spectral sharpening, the results are worse than the images created by other fusion techniques. As seen from the results shown in Figure 4c,d, these images are dominated by the characteristics of the SAR image. It is possible to observe only some separations of the larch forest, and other forest types are almost not distinguishable on these images. In the case of the wavelet-based fusion, the integrated image (Figure 4e) demonstrated a better result compared to the results of the Gram-Schmidt fusion and color normalization spectral sharpening. On this image, larch, cedar, pine and spruce forest types could be distinguished by their spectral properties. Additionally, it could be seen that the image illustrates good textural differentiation between different forest types. In the case of the Ehlers fusion, the fused image (Figure 3f) demonstrated a better result compared to some other combinations, but it had a blurred appearance due to speckle noise. However, on this image it is possible to observe some spectral separations among larch, cedar, spruce and pine forests. Figure 4 shows the comparison of the images obtained by the selected fusion methods.

Evaluation of Features and Standard Classification

At the beginning, in order to define the sites for the training signature selection, from the multisensor images, several areas of interest (AOI)s representing the selected forest classes (i.e., larch, cedar, pine, birch and spruce) have been selected through thorough analysis using a polygon-based approach. For the selection of the sites of training samples, the images obtained by the modifiedIHS transformation, PCA and wavelet-based method have been compared. The separability of the training signatures was first checked in feature space. If the signatures are overlapped in feature space, then they are not separable (Figure 5a). If they are separable, there is no overlap between the signatures (Figure 5b). After checking the signatures in feature space, they were evaluated using Jeffries–Matusita distance. The values of Jeffries–Matusita distance range from 0 to 2.0 and indicate how well the selected pairs are statistically separate. The values greater than 1.9 indicate that the pairs have good separability [30]. After the investigation, the samples that demonstrated the greatest separability were chosen to form the final signatures. The final signatures included 3923 pixels for larch forest, 2535 pixels for cedar forest, 124 pixels for pine forest, 802 pixels for spruce forest and 320 pixels for birch forest. As seen from the separabilities measured by Jeffries–Matusita distance (Table 3), the available forest classes have high statistical overlaps.

Table 3. The separabilities measured by Jeffries–Matusita distance

	Birch	Larch	Pine	Spruce	Cedar
Birch	0.000	1.600	1.856	1.980	1.975
Larch	1.600	0.000	1.594	1.698	1.697
Pine	1.856	1.594	0.000	1.446	1.507
Spruce	1.980	1.698	1.446	0.000	1.235
Cedar	1.975	1.697	1.507	1.235	0.000

In many cases, forest types have similar spectral characteristics and it is not easy to separate them by the use of ordinary feature combinations or fusing techniques. For the successful extraction of the forest classes, reliable features derived from multiple sources should be used. In the case of the present study, texture features might be considered as additional sources. For the classification, the following feature combinations were used:

The original five spectral bands of the Landsat TM data.
The green, red, near infrared and middle infrared (2-5) bands of the Landsat TM data.
The HH polarization component of Envisat SAR and original five spectral bands of the Landsat TM data.
The PC1, PC2 and PC3 of the PCA.
The PC1, PC2, PC3, PC4 and PC5 of the PCA.
The PC1, PC2, PC3, PC4, PC5, PC6 and PC7 of the PCA.
Multiple bands including the original Envisat SAR and Landsat TM data as well as three texture images.
Fuzzy convolution applied to the classification result of the multiple bands that include the original SAR, Landsat TM and three texture images.

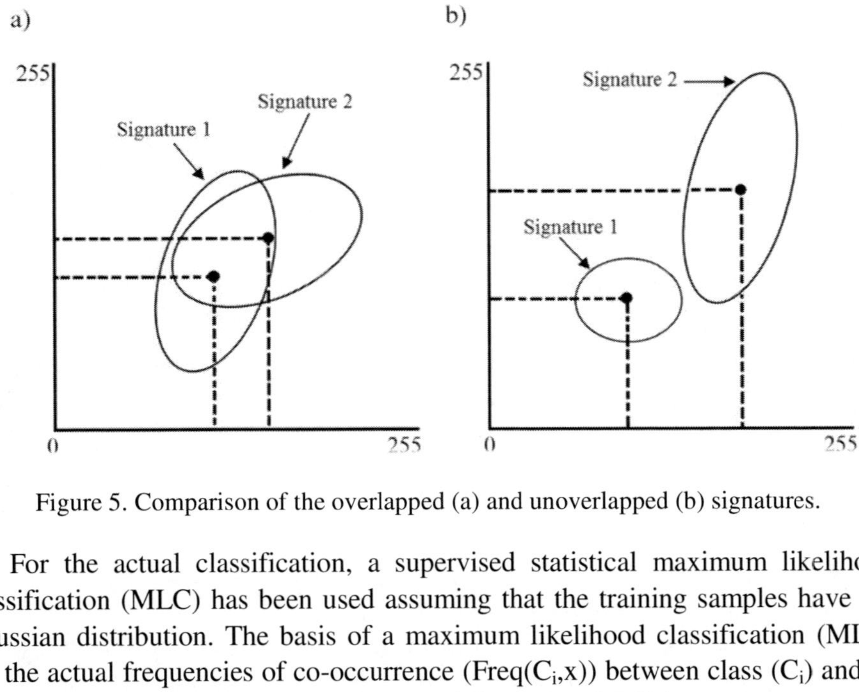

Figure 5. Comparison of the overlapped (a) and unoverlapped (b) signatures.

For the actual classification, a supervised statistical maximum likelihood classification (MLC) has been used assuming that the training samples have the Gaussian distribution. The basis of a maximum likelihood classification (MLC) are the actual frequencies of co-occurrence ($Freq(C_i,x)$) between class (C_i) and an observation vector (x). In the case of multidimensional RS data, we assume that each observation x (pixel) consists of a set of measurements on N variables (features) [28]. The decision rule, assuming Bayes' rule, can be written as follows:

$$P(C_i|x) = P(x|C_i) \bullet P(C_i)/P(x) \quad (1)$$

$P(x|C_i)$ is approximated by a multivariate normal probability density function and it is scaled by a priori probability ($P(C_i)$). This function has as parameters a mean vector (m_i) and covariance matrix (Σ_i) for each class (C_i). These parameters have to be estimated on the basis of a training set or clusters. The formula for the approximation is expressed as follows:

$$P(X|Ci) = (2\pi)^{-\frac{N}{2}} \left|\sum{}_i\right|^{-\frac{1}{2}} \exp\{-\frac{1}{2}(x-m_i)^t \sum{}_i^{-1}(x-m_i)\} \tag{2}$$

$P(C_i)$ is defined by the user's prior knowledge about the area.

$P(x)$ is the probability of finding a pixel from any class and expressed as:

$$P(x) = \sum_{i=1}^{n} P(x \mid Ci) \bullet P(Ci) \tag{3}$$

The actual classification is performed according to $P(C_i|x) > P(C_j|x)$ for all $j \neq i$.

However, $P(x)$ is common to all classes and is usually dropped from the actual classification. In this case, for the classification, the following discriminant function is used:

$$g_i(x) = Ln\{P(x|Ci)\} + Ln\{P(Ci)\} \tag{4}$$

In many cases, the users assume that the classes have equal prior probabilities. In this case, $P(C_i)$ can also be dropped and the discriminant function can be written as follows:

$$g_i(x) = Ln\{P(x|Ci)\} \tag{5}$$

and the classification is performed according to $g_i(x)>g_j(x)$ for all $j \neq i$.

The rule has the maximum benefit of correct classification; that is,a pixel classified by this method has the maximum probability of correct assignment. Therefore, the method is considered as one of the most efficient methods for statistical pattern recognition [41].

For the accuracy assessment, the overall performance has been used. This approach creates a confusion matrix in which reference pixels are compared with the classified pixels and as a result an accuracy report is generated indicating the percentages of the overall accuracy [42]. Forground truth information, different regions containing purest pixels have been selected. The regions were selected on a principle that there were more available pixels to be selected for the evaluation of the larger classes, such as larch and cedar forests, than the smaller classes such as pine and birch forests.

Classification Result Using Original Five Spectral Bands

The MLC of the Bogdkhan Mountain has been performed using the original five spectral bands of the Landsat TM data.

Table 4. The overall classification accuracy of the classified image

	Birch	Larch	Pine	Spruce	Cedar
Birch	201	813	2	0	2
Larch	16	4328	17	26	42
Pine	8	573	52	33	112
Spruce	0	147	2	594	246
Cedar	0	38	51	146	2122

Overall Accuracy = (7297/9571) 76.24%.

Figure 6. Classification result using original five spectral bands.

The decision-rule used the signatures defined from the signature evaluation process (i.e., 3923 pixels for larch forest, 2535 pixels for cedar forest, 124 pixels for pine forest, 802 pixels for spruce forest and 320 pixels for birch forest) and assumed that the selected classes have equal prior probabilities. The final classified image is shown in Figure 6. The overall classification accuracy for the selected classes is shown in Table 4. Asseen from the classification result, the accuracy of the MLC is not high (i.e., 76.24%) and there are high mixtures among birch, larch, cedar and spruce forests.

Classification Result Using Green, Red, Near Infrared and First Middle Infrared Bands

The classification of the test area has been made using the green, red, near infrared and first middle infrared bands of the Landsat TM data. The decision-rule used the same signatures defined from the signature evaluation process and the same assumption of equal prior probabilities. The final classified image is shown in Figure 7. As seen from the classified image, the result is very similar to the result obtained by the use of the original five spectral bands.

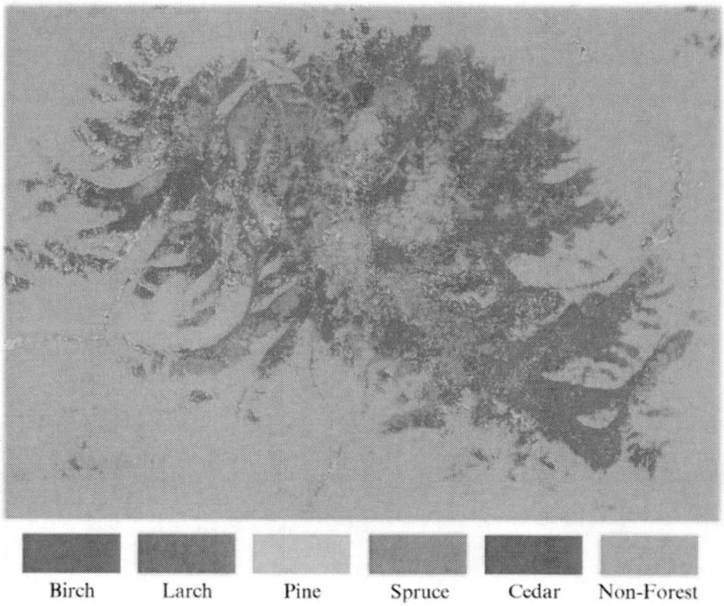

Figure 7. Classification result using four spectral bands.

Table 5. The overall classification accuracy of the classified image

	Birch	Larch	Pine	Spruce	Cedar
Birch	200	811	4	0	3
Larch	15	4335	14	30	46
Pine	10	563	49	31	49
Spruce	0	163	3	592	252
Cedar	0	30	54	145	2177

Overall accuracy = (7353/9576)76.78%.

The overall classification accuracy for the selected five forest classes is shown in Table 5. It has been evaluated using the same set of regions containing the purest pixels as in the previous classification, and it demonstrated an overall accuracy of 76.78%.As could be seen from the confusion matrix shown in Table 5, the performance of the MLC is better than the previous case and it has a tiny improvement. In many cases, users and analysts expect that the addition of more spectral bands would increase the classification accuracy. However, the current study indicates that it is not always true. This is due to a fact that the inclusion of more bands may result in a signature overlap in multidimensional feature space. Therefore, in some cases it is desirable to select a few less-correlated bands.

Classification Result Using SAR and Original Five Spectral Bands

The MLC of the test site has been performed using the HH polarization component of Envisat SAR and original five spectral bands of the Landsat TM data.

Table 6. The overall classification accuracy of the classified image

	Birch	Larch	Pine	Spruce	Cedar
Birch	206	762	2	0	2
Larch	11	4413	6	23	59
Pine	7	551	79	29	127
Spruce	0	134	5	564	179
Cedar	1	48	32	184	2163

Overall Accuracy = (7425/9587) 77.45%.

The result of the classification is shown in Figure 8. As seen from the classified image, the result looks similar to the results obtained by the use of original Landsat TM bands. However, the confusion matrix (Table 6) indicated an overall accuracy of 77.45%. This means that the combined use of optical and microwave data sets produced a better result than the single source image, but the result is still insufficient.

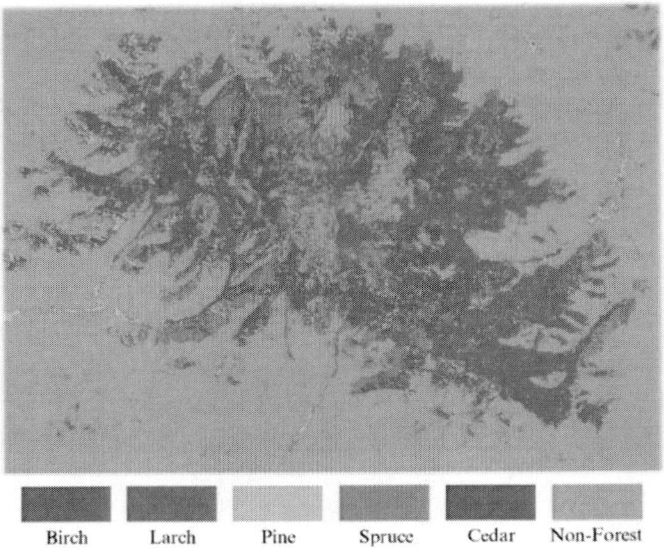

Figure 8. Classification result using SAR and five spectral bands.

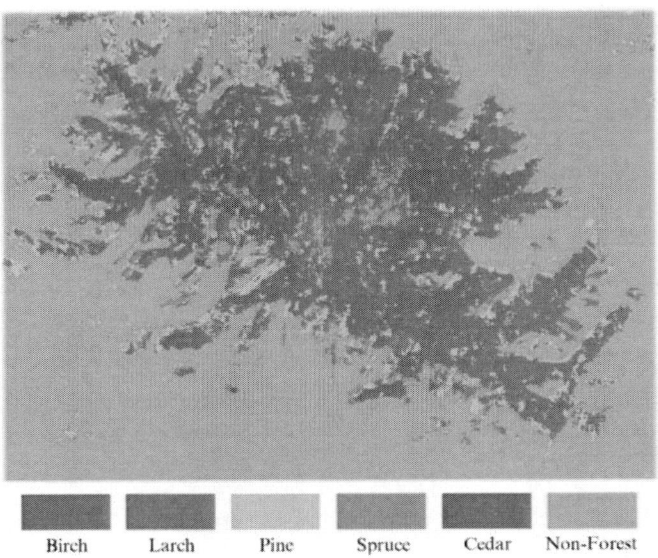

Figure 9. Classification result using the first three PCs.

Classification Result Using the First Three PCs

As it was seen from Table 2, the PC1, PC2 and PC3 of the PCA included 94.32% of the overall variance.

Figure 10. Classification result using the first five PCs.

Table 7. The overall classification accuracy of the classified image

	Birch	Larch	Pine	Spruce	Cedar
Birch	183	2053	13	32	7
Larch	26	3145	15	51	74
Pine	11	480	51	116	67
Spruce	4	104	9	162	100
Cedar	1	114	36	433	2286

Overall Accuracy = (5827/9573) 60.86%.

In many PC-based image analysis, the selection of the first three PCs may be sufficient, if their overall variance exceeds 95%. In the case of the present study, as the overall variance almost reached that level, the PC1, PC2 and PC3 were classified using the MLC. Figure 9 shows the result of the classification and Table

7 indicates the overall accuracy. As seen from the results, the MLC of the first three PCs gives the worst result, because there are different mixtures among all classes. Specifically, there are high mixtures among the birch, larch and spruce forests. Also, many pixels belonging to the pine forest have been misclassified. This indicates that it is not necessary for the first three PCs to produce an improved classification result.

Table 8. The overall classification accuracy of the classified image

	Birch	Larch	Pine	Spruce	Cedar
Birch	204	1013	6	2	2
Larch	17	4133	15	29	42
Pine	1	546	66	17	135
Spruce	0	173	4	540	162
Cedar	3	46	33	211	2191

Overall Accuracy =(7134/9591) 74.38%.

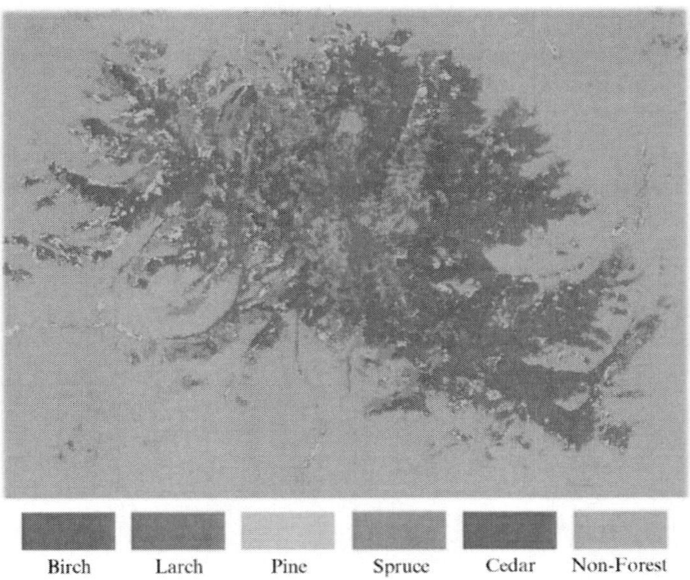

Figure 11. Classification result using the first seven PCs.

Classification Result Using the First FivePCs

As could be seen from Table 2, thePC1, PC2, PC3, PC4 and PC5 of the PCA included 98.59% of the overall variance. The result of the classification is shown in Figure 10 and the overall accuracy is illustrated in Table 8. As seen from the results, there is a significant improvement in the classification performance. For example, there are reduced mixtures among the forest classes compared to the case of the first three PCs. The PCA indicated that there was addition of only 4.27% in the overall variance, but the substantial improvement occurred in the classification accuracy.

Classification Result Using the First Seven PCs

As could be seen from Table 2, the first seven PCs included 99.91%of the overall variance (i.e., it exceeds the overall variance of the first five PCs by only 1.32%).

Table 9. The overall classification accuracy of the classified image

	Birch	Larch	Pine	Spruce	Cedar
Birch	206	488	1	0	0
Larch	17	4708	6	30	54
Pine	0	489	89	20	208
Spruce	0	179	3	563	128
Cedar	2	44	25	186	2143

Overall Accuracy = (7709/9589)80.39%.

The chosen PCs have been classified using the MLC and the result is shown in Figure 11. The confusion matrix (Table 9) indicated an overall accuracy of 80.39%, indicating an improvement occurred in the classification performance compared to the previously classified PC images. As could be seen from the PCA, the first five PCs weredominated by different characteristics of the near infrared, middle infrared, SAR and two texture features and their classification accuracy was not high enough. This was due to a fact that these bands composed of different features with a variety of different characteristics could not create orthogonal features in a multidimensional feature space. When the PC6 and PC7, dominated by the negative characteristics of the correlation filter and visible bands of the Landsat TM, have been added to the first five PCs, the overall classification accuracy was increased by 6.01%. This means that some useful information might be included in the last PCs that contain a negligible part of the overall variance. In the present study, due to the addition of the PC6 and PC7 (i.e., the overall variance has been increased by only 1.32%), the classification accuracy was increased from 74.38% to 80.39%.

Classification Result Using Original SAR, Landsat TM and Three Texture Images

In most cases, for the successful classification of the statistically overlapping classes, reliable additionalfeatures derived from multiple sources should be used in a decision-making process. In the current study, the texture images derived from the original SAR band, could be considered such additional features. The classification of the Bogdkhan Mountain has been performed using all 9 bands. The result of the MLC is shown in Figure 12 and the overallclassification accuracy is illustrated in Table 10.

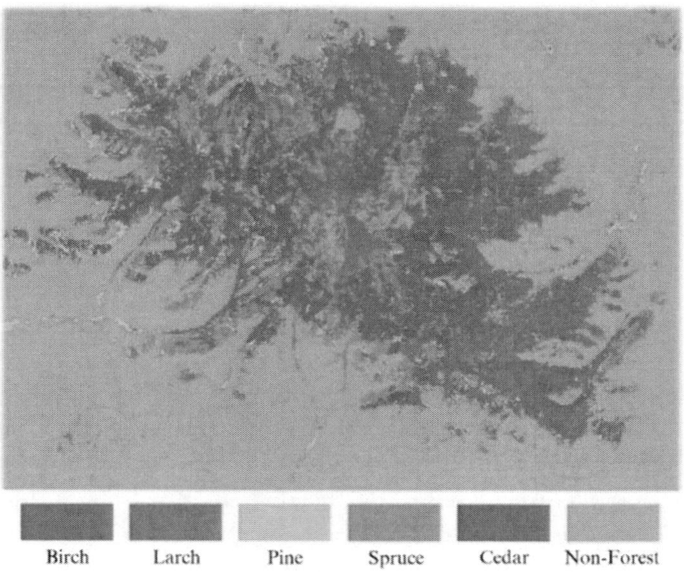

Figure 12. Classification result using multiple bands.

The classification results indicated that some improvements occurred in the overall accuracy of the MLC compared to the classification result of the first seven PCs. For example, in the case of the first seven PCs (Table 9), 488 pixels belonging to the larch forest and 208 pixels of the cedar forest have been classified as birch and pine forests, while in the classification of multiple bands

(Table 10) 352 and 154 pixels of the same forest classes were misclassified as the birch and pine forests. Likewise, 489 pixels of the larch forest of the classified PC image have been misclassified as pine forest, whereas 275 pixels of the same class were classified as the pine forest.

As seen from the comparison of the classified images, the overall accuracies could be improved by adding some orthogonal features to the original data. In the case of the present study, the texture features played a role of the orthogonal features and made the selected signatures of classes more separable in a multidimensional feature space.

Table 10. The overall classification accuracy of the classified image

	Birch	Larch	Pine	Spruce	Cedar
Birch	214	352	1	0	0
Larch	9	5126	3	19	65
Pine	1	275	97	17	154
Spruce	0	116	2	581	130
Cedar	1	37	21	182	2184

Overall Accuracy = (8202/9587) 85.55%.

Table 11. The overall classification accuracy of the classified image

	Birch	Larch	Pine	Spruce	Cedar
Birch	223	197	0	0	0
Larch	2	5496	0	15	32
Pine	0	141	103	9	142
Spruce	0	68	1	582	151
Cedar	0	4	20	193	2208

Overall Accuracy = (8612/9587) 89.83%.

Classification Result Using Fuzzy Convolution

In some cases, to increase the reliability of the classification of the initially classified images, fuzzy convolutions of different sizes can be applied. The fuzzy convolution creates a thematic layer by calculating the total weighted inverse distance of all the classes in a determined window of pixels and assigning the central pixel the class with the largest total inverse distance summed over the entire set of fuzzy classification layers, i.e., classes with a very small distance value will remain unchanged while the classes with higher distance values might change to a neighboring value if there are a sufficient number of neighboring pixels with class values and small corresponding distance values [30].In this study, a fuzzy convolution with a 3x3 size window has been applied to the classification result of the multiple bands.

Figure 13. Classification result using fuzzy convolution.

The classified image is shown in Figure 13. The initial visual inspection of the fuzzy convolved image indicated that there are some improvements on the borders of the neighboring classes that influence the separation of the decision boundaries. The confusion matrix (Table 11) indicated an overall classification accuracy of89.83%. It is seen that the classification accuracy can be improved by the use of fuzzy convolution. As could be seen from the overall classification results, although the combined use of optical, SAR and texture features produced a better result, it is still very difficult to obtain a reliable forest map by the use of the standard technique.

The Refined Classification Method

For several decades, single-source multispectral data sets have been effectively used for forest mapping. Unlike single-source data, multisource data sets have proved to offer better potential for discriminating between different forest classes.

Generally, it is very important to design a suitable image processing procedure in order to successfully classify any RS data into a number of class labels. The effective use of different features derived from multiple sources and the selection of a reliable classification technique can be a key significance for the improvement of classification accuracy [43]. In this study, for the classification of forest classes, a refined MLC algorithm has been constructed. As the features, the multiple bands that include the original optical and SAR as well as three texture images have been used.

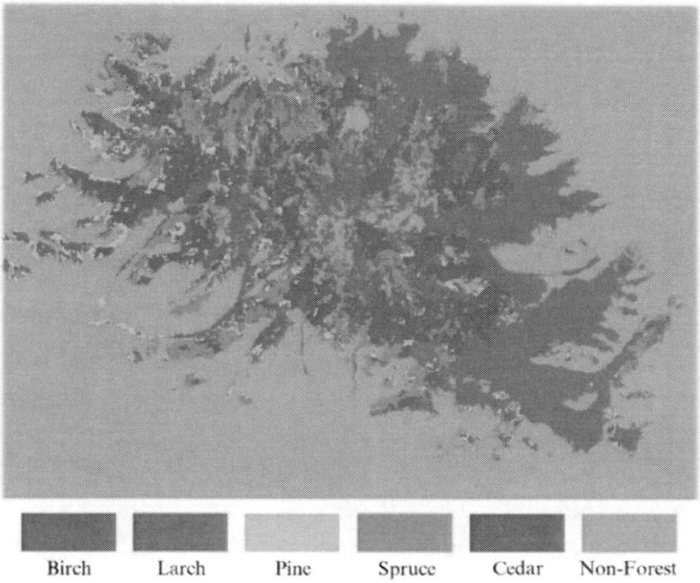

Figure 14. Classification result using the refined classification.

Unlike the traditional MLC, the constructed classification algorithm uses spatial thresholds defined from the contextual knowledge. The contextual knowledge is based on the spectral and textural variations of the available forest classes in different parts of the fused images and the thresholds are applied to separate the statistically overlapping classes. It is clear that a spectral classifier will be ineffective if applied to the statistically overlapping classes because they have very similar spectral characteristics. For such spectrally mixed classes, classification accuracies should be improved if the spatial properties of the classes of objects could be incorporated into the classification criteria. The idea of the spatial threshold is that it uses a polygon boundary to separate the overlapping classes and only the pixels falling within the threshold boundary are used for the classification.

In that case, the likelihood of the pixels to be correctly classified will significantly increase, because the pixels belonging to the class that overlaps with the class to be classified using the threshold boundary are temporarily excluded from the decision making process. In such a way, the image can be classified several times using different threshold boundaries and the results can be merged [44].

Table 12. The overall classification accuracy of the classified image

	Birch	Larch	Pine	Spruce	Cedar
Birch	223	95	0	0	0
Larch	2	5703	0	8	17
Pine	0	71	113	4	95
Spruce	0	33	0	689	80
Cedar	0	4	11	98	2341

Overall Accuracy =(9069/9587) 94.59%.

The result of the classification using the refined method is shown in Figure 14. For the accuracy assessment of the classification result, the overall performance has been used, taking the same number of sample points as in the multiple bands. The confusion matrix produced for the refined classification showed an overall accuracy of94.59% (Table 12). As could be seen from Figure 14, the result of the classification using the refined MLC method is better than the result of the standard method. A general diagram of the refined classification technique is shown is Figure 15.

Update of Forest GIS

GIS is a computer-based system capable of capturing, storing, analyzing, and displaying geographically referenced information – the information attached to a location [45]. The most commonly used method of data capturing is the digitization, where hard copy maps or survey plans are transferred into digital formats through the use of special software programs and spatial-referencing capabilities. With the emergence of modern ortho-rectified images acquired from both space and air platforms, heads-up digitizing is becoming the main approach through which positional data are extracted [46]. Compared to the traditional method of tracing, heads-up digitizing involves the tracing of spatial data directly on top of the acquired imagery. Thus, due to rapid development in science and technology, primary spatial data acquisition within a GIS is becoming more and more sophisticated.

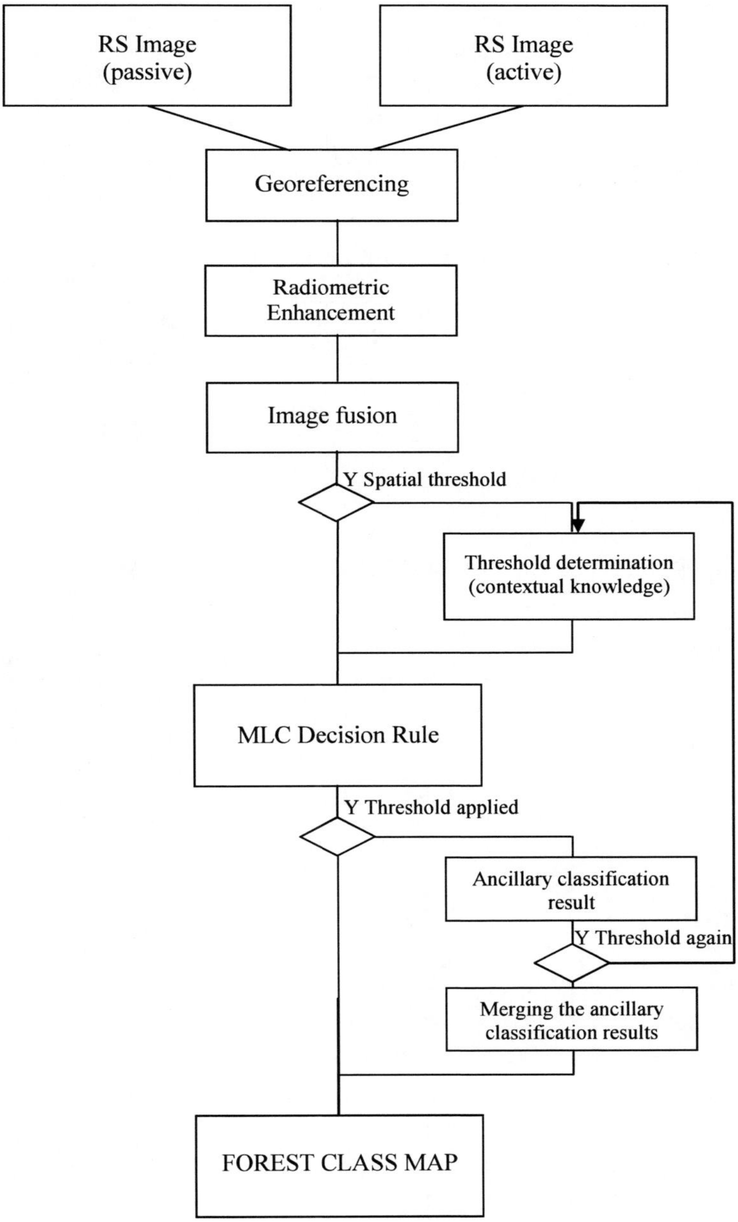

Figure 15. A general diagram for the refined classification.

(Table 10) 352 and 154 pixels of the same forest classes were misclassified as the birch and pine forests. Likewise, 489 pixels of the larch forest of the classified PC image have been misclassified as pine forest, whereas 275 pixels of the same class were classified as the pine forest.

As seen from the comparison of the classified images, the overall accuracies could be improved by adding some orthogonal features to the original data. In the case of the present study, the texture features played a role of the orthogonal features and made the selected signatures of classes more separable in a multidimensional feature space.

Table 10. The overall classification accuracy of the classified image

	Birch	Larch	Pine	Spruce	Cedar
Birch	214	352	1	0	0
Larch	9	5126	3	19	65
Pine	1	275	97	17	154
Spruce	0	116	2	581	130
Cedar	1	37	21	182	2184

Overall Accuracy = (8202/9587) 85.55%.

Table 11. The overall classification accuracy of the classified image

	Birch	Larch	Pine	Spruce	Cedar
Birch	223	197	0	0	0
Larch	2	5496	0	15	32
Pine	0	141	103	9	142
Spruce	0	68	1	582	151
Cedar	0	4	20	193	2208

Overall Accuracy = (8612/9587) 89.83%.

Classification Result Using Fuzzy Convolution

In some cases, to increase the reliability of the classification of the initially classified images, fuzzy convolutions of different sizes can be applied. The fuzzy convolution creates a thematic layer by calculating the total weighted inverse distance of all the classes in a determined window of pixels and assigning the central pixel the class with the largest total inverse distance summed over the entire set of fuzzy classification layers, i.e., classes with a very small distance value will remain unchanged while the classes with higher distance values might change to a neighboring value if there are a sufficient number of neighboring pixels with class values and small corresponding distance values [30]. In this analysis. Over the past few years, RS techniques and technologies, including system capabilities have been significantly improved. Meanwhile, the costs for the primary RS data sets have drastically decreased [48]. This means that it is possible to extract from RS images different types of forest related information in a cost-effective way and update layers within a GIS.

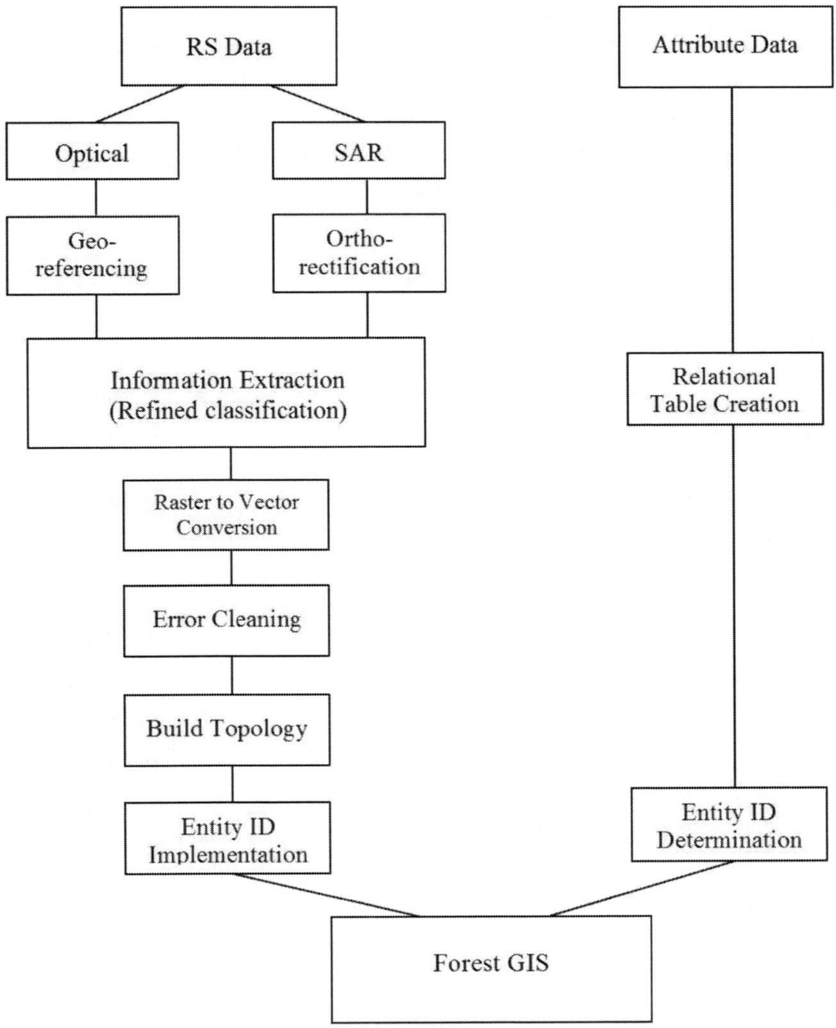

Figure 17. A diagram for update of forest GIS via processing of multisource RS images.

In the present study, it was assumed that there is an operational forest GIS that stores historical thematic layers and there was a need to update a forest class layer. The forest inventory data for the Bogdkhan Mountain was last updated in 1988. Therefore, the current layer was created using an existing forest taxonomy map of 1988 and the ArcGIS system was used for its digitizing. The digitized map is shown in Figure 16. As the overall classification accuracy of the classified multisource images exceeds 90%, the result can be directly used to update the layer of the operational GIS. For this end, a raster thematic map (i.e., classified image) extracted from the multisource RS data sets should be converted to a vector structure. After error cleaning and editing, the converted from raster to vector layer can be topologically structured and stored within the forest GIS. If one compares the forest layers created from the forest taxonomy map and classified RS image, could see what changes had occurred. A diagram for the update of a forest class layer of a GIS via processing of multisource RS images is shown in Figure 17.

Conclusion

The overall aimof this chapter was to evaluate the performances of different image fusion techniques for the enhancement of spectral and textural variations of different forest typesto be used for the training site selection and apply arefined classification method for the extraction of forest class informationfrom the multisource images in order to update a forest GIS. For the test area, Bogdkhan Mountain situated in the central part of Mongolia and one of the world's oldest and officially protected sites, was selected.As the fusion techniques,modified IHS transformation, PCA technique, Gram-Schmidt method, color normalization spectral sharpening, wavelet-based fusion, and Ehlers method were used. Of these methods, the modifiedIHS transformation, PCA, and wavelet-based fusion gave better results compared to the other fusion techniques in terms of the spatial and spectral separations among different forest types. For the classification of the multisource images, the statistical MLC and refined method were used and the results were compared. In order to evaluate the classification accuracy of different features, the feature combinations were classified using the standard method. When the results were compared, the classification of the multiple bands, which included the original optical, SAR, and three texture images,gave the superior result. The constructed refined classification method used spatial thresholds defined from contextual knowledge and multiple features obtained through a feature derivation process. As could be seen from the classification results, the performance of the refined classification was much better than the performances of the standard method and the output could be directly used to update forest GIS. Overall, the research indicated that multisource information can improve the interpretation and classification of forest classes and the elaborated refined classification method is a powerful tool in the production of a reliable forest map.

References

[1] Enkhjargal, D., Amarsaikhan, D., Battsengel, V. and Tsogzol, G. (2014). Applications of multitemporal optical images for forest resources study in Mongolia. In: *CD-ROM Proceedings of the ACRS*, Nay Pyi Taw, Myanmar, October 2014.

[2] Almeida, R., Shimabukuro, Y. E., Rosenqvist, A. and Sanchez, G. A. (2009). Using dual-polarized ALOS PALSAR data for detecting new fronts of deforestation in the Brazilian Amazonia. *International Journal of Remote Sensing*, Vol.30 (14), pp.3735-3743.

[3] Amarsaikhan, D., Battsengel, V., Amarjargal, Sh., Egshiglen, E., Ganzorig, M. and Enkhjargal, D. (2011). Applications of optical and microwave RS for forest mapping in Mongolia. In: *CD-ROM Proceedings of the ACRS*, Taipei, Taiwan, October 2011.

[4] Ferreira, L. G., Ferreira, N. C., Huete, A. R. and Ferreira, M. E. (2007). An operational deforestation mapping using MODIS data and spatial context analysis. *International Journal of Remote Sensing*, Vol. 28(1), pp.47-62.

[5] Badarinath, K. V. S., Sharma, A. R. and Kharol, S.K. (2011). *Forest fire monitoring and burnt area mapping using satellite data: a study over the forest region of Kerala State, India.* Vol. 32(1), pp.85-102.

[6] Matricardi, E. A. T., Skole, D. L., Pedlowski, M. A. and Chomentowski. (2013). *Assessment of forest disturbances by selective logging and forest fires in the Brazilian Amazon using Landsat data.* Vol. 34(4), pp.1057-1086.

[7] Todd, A., Schroeder, T. A., Healey, S. P., Moisen, G. G., Frescino, T. S., Cohen, W. B., Huang, Ch., Kennedy, R. E. and Yan, Zh. (2014).Improving estimates of forest disturbance by combating observations from Landsat time series with US Forest Service Forest Inventory and Analysis data. *Remote Sensing of Environment*, Vol.154, pp.61-73.

[8] Amarsaikhan, D., Ganzorig, M., Batbayar, G., Narangerel, D. and Tumentsetseg, Sh. (2004). An integrated approach of optical and SAR images for forest change study. *Asian Journal of Geoinformatics*, Vol. 4(3), pp. 27-33.

[9] Huang, Sh., Crabtree, R. L., Potter, Ch. and Gross, P. (2009).Estimating the quantity and quality of coarse woody debris in Yellowstone post-fire forest ecosystem from fusion of SAR and optical data. *Remote Sensing of Environment*, Vol. 113(9), pp.1926-1938.

[10] Morel, A. C., Fisher, J. B. and Malhi, Y. (2012). *Evaluating the potential to monitor aboveground biomass in forest and oil palm in Sabah, Malaysia, for 2000-2008 with Landsat ETM+ and ALOS-PALSAR.* Vol. 33(11), pp. 3614-3639.

[11] Hoan, N. T., Tateishi, R., Alsaaideh, B., Ngigi, T., Alimuddin, I. and Johnson, B. (2013). Tropical mapping using a combination and microwave data of ALOS. *International Journal of Remote Sensing,* Vol. 34(1), pp.139-153.

[12] Sybrand V. B., Comber, A. and Lamb, A. (2014).Random forest classification of salt marsh vegetation habitats using quad-polarimetric airborne SAR, elevation and optical RS data. *Remote Sensing of Environment*, Vol.149, pp. 118-129.

[13] Amarsaikhan, D., Saandar, M., Battsengel, V. and Amarjargal, Sh. (2012b). Forest resources study in Mongolia using advanced spatial technologies. *International Archives of the Photogrammetry, RS and Spatial Information Sciences, Vol. XXXIX-B7, XXII ISPRS Congress,* Melbourne, Australia.

[14] Amarsaikhan, D. and Douglas, T. (2004). Data fusion and multisource data classification. *International Journal of Remote Sensing,* No.17, Vol. 25, pp.3529-3539.

[15] Zhang, J. (2010), Multi-source remote sensing data fusion: status and trends. *International Journal of Image and Data Fusion*, 1, pp.5 – 24.

[16] Sritarapipat, T., Kasetkasem, T. and Rakwatin, P. (2014). Fusion and registration of THEOS multispectral and panchromatic images. *International Journal of Remote Sensing*, Vol. 35(13), pp.5120-5147.

[17] Karathanassi, V., Kolokousis, P. and Ioannidou, S. (2007).A comparison study on fusion methods using evaluation indicators. *International Journal of Remote Sensing*, Vol. 28, pp.2309 – 2341.

[18] Ehlers, M., Klonus, S. and Åstrand, P. J. (2008).Quality Assessment for multi-sensor multi-date image fusion, CD-ROM *Proceedings of ISPRS Congresses*, Beijing, China, July 3- 11, 2008.

[19] Fang, F., Li, F., Zhang, G. and Shen, C. (2013). A variational method for multisource remote-sensing image fusion. *International Journal of Remote Sensing*, Vol. 34(7), pp.2470–2486.

[20] Amarsaikhan, D. (2013). Environmental studies of Mongolia using RS and GIS techniques. *Proceedings of the International Conference* on Climate Changein Arid and Semi-Arid Region, Ulaanbaatar, Mongolia, pp.18-26.

[21] Kuplich, T.M., Freitas, C.C. and Soares, J.V. (2000).The study of ERS-1 SAR and Landsat TM synergism for land use classification. *International Journal of Remote Sensing,* Vol.21(10), pp. 2101-2111.

[22] Hyde, P., Dubayah, R., Walker, W., Blair, J. B., Hofton, M. and Hunsaker, C. (2006). Mapping forest structure for wildlife habitat analysis using multi-sensor (LiDAR, SAR/InSAR, ETM+, Quickbird) synergy. *Remote Sensing of Environment*, Vol. 102(1–2), pp.63-73.

[23] Cartus, O., Santoro, M., Schmullius, Ch. and Li, Z. (2011).Large area forest stem volume mapping in the boreal zone using synergy of ERS-1/2 tandem coherence and MODIS vegetation continuous fields. *Remote Sensing of Environment*, Vol. 115(3), pp.931-943.

[24] Dong, J., Xiao, X., Sheldon, S., Biradar, C., Duong, N. D.and Hazarika, M. (2012). A comparison of forest maps in Mainland Southeast Asia from multiple sources: PALSAR, MERIS, MODIS and ERA. *Remote Sensing of Environment*, Vol. 127, pp.60-73.

[25] Laurin, G. V., Liesenberg, V., Chen, Q., Guerriero, L., Frate, F. D., Bartolini, A., Coomes, D., Wilebore, B., Lindsell, J. and Valentini, R. (2013). Optical and SAR sensor synergies for forest and land cover mapping in a tropical site in West Africa. *International Journal of Applied Earth Observation and Geoinformation*, Vol.21, pp.7-16.

[26] Amarsaikhan, D., Ganzorig, M., Saandar, M., Blotevogel, H. H.,Egshiglen, E., Gantuya, R., Nergui, B. and Enkhjargal, D. (2012a).Comparison of multisource image fusion methods and land cover classification. *International Journal of Remote Sensing,* Vol. 33(8), pp.2532-2550.

[27] UNESCO. (1996). Mongolia Sacred Mountains: Bogd Khan, Burkhan Khaldun, Otgon Tenger, UNESCO World Heritage Center, available at http://whc.unesco.org/en/tentativelists/936.

[28] Amarsaikhan, D. and Sato, M. (2004).Validation of the Pi-SAR data for land cover mapping. *Journal of the Remote Sensing Society of Japan, No.2,* Vol. 24, pp.133-139.

[29] Serkan, M., Musaoglu, N., Kirkici, H. and Ormeci, C. (2008). Edge and fine detail preservation in SAR images through speckle reduction with an adaptive mean filter. *International Journal of Remote Sensing,* Vol. 29(23), pp. 6727 – 6738.

[30] ERDAS, (2010). New ERDAS Field Guide, *ERDAS*, Inc. Atlanta, Georgia, pp.776.

[31] ENVI, (2004). User's Guide, Research Systems Inc.

[32] Pohl, C. and Van Genderen, J. L. (1998). Multisensor image fusion in remote sensing: concepts, methods and applications. *International Journal of Remote Sensing,* Vol.19, 9, pp.823–854.

[33] Amarsaikhan, D., Bolorchuluun, Ch., Narangerel, Z. and Gantuya, R. (2009). Integration of RS and GIS for forest monitoring in Mongolia. In: *CD-ROM Proceedings of the Asian Conference on RS*, Beijing, China, October 2009.

[34] Jiang, D., Zhuang, D., Huang, Y. and Fu, J. (2011). Survey of multispectral image fusion techniques in remote sensing applications. *Image Fusion and Its Applications*, In Tech Open Access, pp.1-22.

[35] Siddiqui, Y. (2003).The modified IHS method for fusing satellite imagery. ASPRS 2003 *Annual Conference Proceedings*, American Society for Photogrammetry and Remote Sensing Anchorage, Alaska (CD publication).

[36] Richards, J. A. (2013). *Remote Sensing Digital Image* Analysis-An Introduction, ISBN-13: 978-3642300615, 5thEdition (Berlin: Springer-Verlag), pp.439.

[37] Laben, C. A., Bernard, V. and Brower, W. (2000). Process for enhancing the spatial resolution of multispectral imagery using pan-sharpening. United States Patent Application No. 6011875.

[38] Vrabel, J. C., Doraiswamy, P., McMurtrey, J. E. and Stern, A. (2002). Demonstration of the accuracy of improved resolution hyperspectral imagery. *Proceedings of SPIE 4725. Algorithms and Technologies for Multispectral, Hyperspectral, and Ultraspectral Imagery* VIII, pp.556–567.

[39] Pajares, G. and Cruz, J.M. (2004).A wavelet-based image fusion, *Pattern Recognition.* Vol. 37(9), pp.1855-1872.

[40] Klonus, S. And Ehlers, M. (2009). Performance of evaluation methods in image fusion, *Proceedings of 12th. International Conference on Information Fusion*, Seattle, USA, pp.1409-1416.

[41] Erbek, F. S., Zkan, C. O., Taberner, M. (2004).Comparison of maximum likelihood classification method with supervised artificial neural network algorithms for land use activities. *International Journal of Remote Sensing,* Vol. 25, pp.1733–1748.

[42] Mather, P. M. and Koch, M. (2010).*Computer Processing of Remotely-Sensed Images: An Introduction*, Fourth Edition, (Wiley, John & Sons).

[43] Lu, D. and Weng, Q. (2007).A survey of image classification methods and techniques for improving classification performance. *International Journal of Remote Sensing,* Vol. 28(5), pp.823-870.

[44] Amarsaikhan, D., Bat-Erdene, Ts., Ganzorig, M. and Nergui, B. (2013). Applications of remote sensing techniques and GIS for urban land change studies in Mongolia. *American Journal of GIS,* 2013. Vol. 2(3), pp.27-36.

[45] Folger, P. (2009).Geospatial information and geographic information systems: Current issues and future challenges. *Congressional Research Service*, CRS Report for Congress, pp.1-30.

[46] Amarsaikhan, D. and Ganzorig, M. (2010). *Principles of GIS for Natural Resources Management, 2nd edn* (Ulaanbaatar: Academic Press).

[47] Hwang, S. (2013).Placing GIS in sustainability education. *Journal of Geography in Higher Education*, Vol. 37(2), pp.276–291.

[48] Amarsaikhan, D. and Saandar, M. (2011).Chapter8 - Fusion of Multisource Images for Update of Urban GIS. *Image Fusion and Its Applications,* In TECH Open Access Publisher, pp.127-152.

Reviewed by Prof. Dr. J. Janzen, Free University of Berlin, Germany

In: Image Fusion
Editor: C. T. Davis, pp. 121-153

ISBN: 978-1-63482-115-5

Chapter 5

MULTIMODAL MEDICAL IMAGE FUSION BASED ON SUSAN FEATURE IN FRAMELET DOMAIN

Gaurav Bhatnagar*
Indian Institute of Technology Jodhpur, Jodhpur, India

Abstract

Multimodal medical image fusion is an important task for the retrieval of complementary information from medical images. In this chapter, a novel framework for multimodal medical image fusion is proposed, which enables the decomposition of input images into low- and high frequency bands using framelet transform and utilizes local visibility and smallest univalue segment assimilating nucleus (SUSAN) features fusion rules for coefficient selection at different levels. The final fused image is obtained from the superposition of selected coefficients in bot low- and high-frequency bands. The fused medical image that is produced by this framework presents a visually better representation than the input images. Experimental results highlights the expediency and suitability of the proposed algorithm and the efficiency is carried by the comparison made between proposed and existing algorithm.

Keywords: Medical image fusion; framelet transform; visibility of image; Smallest univalue segment assimilating nucleus

*E-mail address: goravb@iitj.ac.in

1. Introduction

With the rapid development in high-tech and advanced instrumentations, medical imaging has become a vital component of a large number of applications, including diagnosis, research, and treatment. This rife development has enabled radiologists to quickly acquire images of the human body and its internal structures with effective resolution and realism. These images are often known as multimodality medical images such as X-ray, computed tomography (CT), magnetic resonance imaging (MRI), magnetic resonance angiography (MRA), and positron emission tomography (PET) images [1]. These multimodality medical images usually provide complementary and occasionally conflicting information. For example, X-ray computed tomography (CT) can provide dense structures like bones and implants with less distortion, but it cannot detect physiological changes [2]. Similarly, normal and pathological soft tissue can be better visualized by magnetic resonance (MR) image and the positive electron tomography (PET) can be used to provide better information on blood flow and flood activity with low spatial resolution. For medical diagnosis, treatment planning and evaluation, the complementary information obtained from different modality images is needed. For example, combined PET/CT imaging can concurrently visualize anatomical and physiological characteristics of the human body and can also be used to view tumor activity in conjunction with anatomical references in oncology. Also in organ diagnosis, the combined PET/CT imaging is very useful, where tumor boundaries are difficult to discern. Therefore, the fusion of the multimodal medical images is necessary and it has become a promising and very challenging research area nowadays. Image fusion can be defined as the process in which some important features of multiple input images are combined into a single image without any loss of information. Medical image fusion aims at integrating complementary as well as redundant information from multiple modality images to obtain a more complete and accurate description of the same object. It provides easy access to the PET/CT/MRI images at the same location where reading from all other modalities is done, allowing radiologists to quickly and efficiently report PET/CT/MRI studies [3]. There are generally two basic requirements for image fusion [4, 5]. The former is that the fused image should possess all possible relevant information contained in the source images whereas the latter states that the fusion process should not introduce any artifact, noise or unexpected feature in the fused image. So far, many effective techniques for image fusion have been proposed in the literature especially for medical image. A detailed literature review on image fusion can be found in Section 2. Some medical applications of image fusion are found in radiology, molecular and brain imaging, oncology, diagnosis of cardiac diseases, neuroradiology and ultrasound [6, 7, 8, 9, 10, 11].

In this chapter, a new multimodal medical image fusion technique using framelet transform is proposed, which is based on multiresolution principle and performed multilevel fusion over low- and high-frequency bands. Two novel fusion rules, based on visibility and smallest univalue segment assimilating nucleus (SUSAN) features, are then proposed for combining the low- and high-frequency bands. These rules preserves more details in source images and further improves the quality of the fused bands. In the final step, the fused image is obtained using inverse framelet transform on the composite frequency bands. Framelet transform is designed by tight frame filter banks, which provides symmetry and shift invariance due to dense plane of the time scale. These properties produce smoother low-frequency and more informative high-frequency sub-bands. The two fusion rules that are employed by considering the physical meaning of the sub-bands. The low-frequency sub-bands are fused by considering the local visibility feature as fusion measure instead of simple averaging as used in the existing schemes. Since the low-frequency sub-band is the original image at coarser resolution level and can be considered as subsampled and smother version of it. Therefore, it carries most of the information of source images. The local visibility tries to select the highest local visibility form the focused regions. In contrast, the high-frequency sub-bands are fused based on texture information obtained from the Smallest Univalue Segment Assimilating Nucleus (SUSAN) feature extractor. Generally, the high-frequency subbands contains the details/texture information of an image. Therefore, a good method for the high-frequency subbands should produce large coefficients on those edges. The SUSAN feature will provide most prominent texture information to select high-frequency coefficients. The fused medical image that is produced by this framework presents a visually better representation than the input images. Experimental results highlights the expediency and suitability of the algorithm and efficiency are carried by the comparison made between proposed and existing algorithm.

Rest of the chapter is organized as follows: Image fusion literature is discussed in Section 2. The framelet transform and the proposed medical image fusion framework are explained in sections 3 and 4 respectively. The experimental results and discussions are presented in section 5. Finally, conclusions of the work are given in Section 6.

2. Existing Works in Medical Image Fusion

In general, there are two stages involved in the medical image fusion methods. The first stage is called image registration, which is the process of correcting the spatial misalignment among the different image modalities. The most common misalignment in the images involve the variability in scale changes, rotations and translations. Registration process generally becomes complicated in the presence of different noises, missing features and outliers in the images. In contrast, the second stage involves the identification and integration of the relevant information, for a given clinical assessment purpose, from all the registered images. So far, many effective techniques for image fusion have been proposed in the literature especially for medical image modalities. The summary of the major medial image fusion methods, the applicable/used modalities and the applications in the medical imaging studies are presented in table 1.

The simplest ways are pixel-by-pixel [12] gray level average or selection of the source images but these ways lead to undesirable side effects such as reduced contrast. Another simple approach includes image fusion methods based on statistical and numerical methods [13]. However, it is quiet difficult to give a generic statistical and numerical process, which will work for all possible image modalities. The morphological methods are highly depend on the structuring operator that defines the opening and closing operations. Therefore, a sequence of operations calculate the scale specific features, which results in high computational complexity. The most common techniques for fusion are multiresolution based fusion, which includes contrast pyramid [18], gradient pyramid [19], wavelet based multiresolution method [18, 19, 20, 21, 22, 23, 24]. These methods produce promising results in less computation time and less memory when compared to others. However, these methods often produce undesirable side effects like block artifacts, reduced contrast etc which often result in the wrong diagnosis. These side effects are due to the drawbacks of wavelet transform such as lack of symmetry, critical sampling and less vanishing moments. These drawbacks are rectified to some extent by using near shift-invariant multiresolution representation like framelet transform [23, 24]. The beyond wavelet-based fusion (such as curvelet [25] and counterlet transform [26, 27, 28]) may improve the performance results, but these transform may lead to greater complexity in computation and parameterization due to the underlying sophisticated process.

Table 1. Multimodal medical image fusion methods with applications

Method	Modalities	Fusion Strategies	Applications
Morphology	MRI, CT	Averaging, maximum, morphology towers, K-L transforms and morphology pyramids	brain diagnosis [14, 15]
Multiresolution Analysis	MRI, CT, PET, Mammogram, MRA, fMRI, SPECT, Ultrasound	Image pyramid, wavelet transform, stationary wavelet transform, lifting wavelet transform, dual tree complex wavelet transform, framelet transform, countourlet transform	medical image pseudo coloring [16], super resolution [17], medical diagnosis [18, 19, 20, 21, 22, 23, 24, 25, 26, 27, 28], segmentation [29], 3D conformal radiotherapy treatment planning [30] and color visualization [31].
Artificial Neural Network	MRI, CT, PET, Mammogram, MRA, fMRI, SPECT, Ultrasound	Neural networks, clustering neural network, fuzzy neural networks, wavelet neural networks	feature generation [32], classification [32], data fusion [32], image fusion [33, 34, 35], microcalcification diagnosis [33], medical diagnosis [34], breast cancer detection [36, 37], classifier fusion [37], cancer diagnosis [38] and natural computing methods [39].
Fuzzy logic	MRI, CT, PET, Mammogram, MRA, fMRI, SPECT, Ultrasound	Image fuzzification, modification of membership values, Image defuzzification, fuzzy combination operators, neuro-fuzzy networks	brain diagnosis [40, 41, 42], cancer treatment [43], image segmentation and integration [43, 44], maximization mutual information [45], deep brain stimulation [46] and brain tumor segmentation [47].
Others	MRI, CT, PET, Mammogram, MRA, fMRI, SPECT, Ultrasound	PCA, ICA, Fuzzy c-means clustering, SVM	Image fusion [48, 49, 50, 51], cancer diagnosis [52], classifier fusion [52, 53], breast cancer tumor [53], tumor segmentation [54], content-based image retrieval [55] and gene classification [56].

The neural network and fuzzy logic based techniques need some manual inputs (such as initial parameters), which ceases their practical aspects. Further, these are also computationally complex due to the long iteration timing and manual parameterization of the artificial neural networks. In others category, principal component analysis (PCA) based methods [48, 50, 51] are well-known and widely used. The PCA based methods gives baseline results relative to other approaches. This was expected because this method has no scale selectivity. In general, the use of near shift-invariant multiresolution representation can be identified as an optimal method and this motivated us to use it for multimodal medical image fusion.

3. Framelet Transform

Framelet transform [57, 58, 59] is very similar to wavelet transform but has some important differences. In particular, framelet transform has one scaling function $\phi(t)$ and two wavelet functions $\psi_1(t)$ and $\psi_2(t)$ whereas wavelet transform has one scaling function $\phi(t)$ and one wavelet function $\psi(t)$.

Let us suppose the low-pass and high pass filters associated with $\phi(t)$, $\psi_1(t)$ and $\psi_2(t)$ are $h_0(n)$, $h_1(n)$ and $h_2(n)$ respectively. The definition of scaling and wavelet functions are given by

$$\phi(t) = \sqrt{2}\sum_n h_0(n)\phi(2t-n) \tag{1}$$

$$\psi_i(t) = \sqrt{2}\sum_n h_i(n)\phi(2t-n),\ i=1,2. \tag{2}$$

Using Eqns. 1 and 2 any function $f(t)$ can be written in the terms of scaling and wavelet functions as a series expansion given by

$$f(t) = \sum_{k=-\infty}^{\infty} c(k)\phi_k(t) + \sum_{i=1}^{2}\sum_{j=0}^{\infty}\sum_{k=-\infty}^{\infty} d_i(j,k)\psi_{i,j,k}(t) \tag{3}$$

where $c(k)$ and $d_i(k,j)$ are the scaling and wavelet coefficients associated with $\phi(t)$ and $\psi_i(t)$ respectively, given by

$$c(k) = \int_{-\infty}^{\infty} f(t)\phi_k(t)dt,\ \ d_i(j,k) = \int_{-\infty}^{\infty} f(t)\psi_{i,j,k}(t)dt \tag{4}$$

The interpretation of framelet transform (Eqn. 3) is same as the wavelet transform i.e. the first summation gives the low-frequency function or coarser approximation of $f(t)$ whereas another summation will give the two high-frequency functions corresponding to $\psi_1(t)$ and $\psi_2(t)$ at scale $j = 0$, the combination of these two summation is called the 1-level framelet transform of $f(t)$. Further, if the value of j increases, high-frequency bands at different levels are obtained to get a multilevel framelet transform structure. Figure 1 shows the 3-level framelet structure for $f(t)$, where $\overline{\phi}(t)$, $\overline{\psi}_1(t)$ and $\overline{\psi}_2(t)$ are the dual functions of $\phi(t)$, $\psi_1(t)$ and $\psi_2(t)$ respectively. The definition of $\phi(t)$, $\psi_1(t)$ and $\psi_2(t)$ suggest that the used fitlerbanks are oversampled. Therefore, the above mentioned structure of framelet transform (figure 1) can be represented in terms of filterbanks and upsampling/downsampling (figure 2).

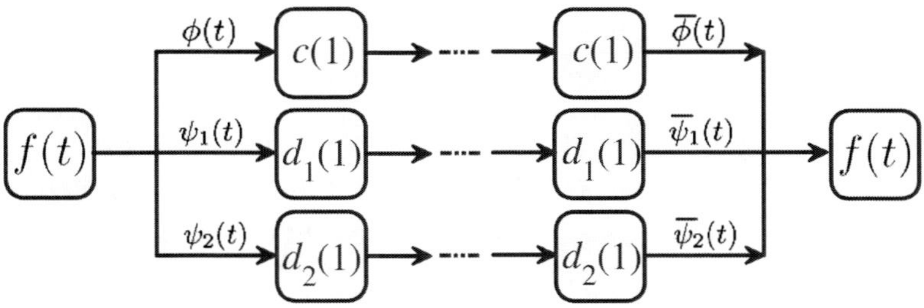

Figure 1. 1-level Framelet Structure of a function $f(t)$.

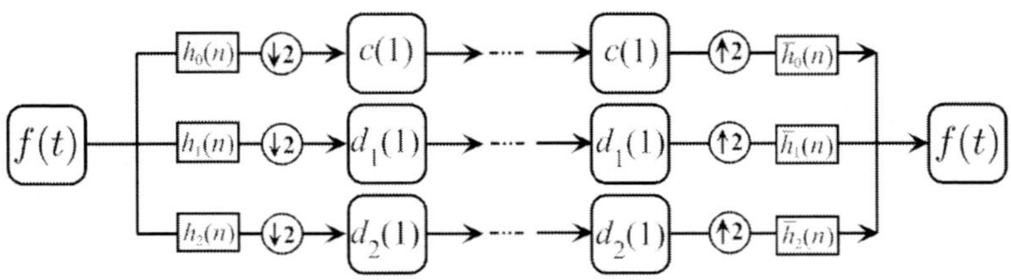

Figure 2. 1-level Framelet Structure of a function $f(t)$ in terms of filterbanks and upsampling/downsampling.

The use of framelet transform has significant advantages over the wavelet like transforms. In fact, framelet transform overcomes the drawbacks of existing wavelet and related transforms in image fusion due to these advantages only. The following advantages of framelet transform acted as the motivation for us to use it for image fusion.

- Framelet transform designs the wavelet tight frames based on iterated oversampled filter banks. The main benefit of tight frames is that the signal is reconstructed with the transpose of the forward transform.
- The framelet transform has FIR perfect reconstruction filter banks which produce reconstructed signals with no or minimal error. Further, framelet transform has more degrees of freedom for design.
- Unlike wavelet related transforms, framelet transform uses one scaling and two wavelet functions where the two wavelets are offset from one another by one half, i.e., the integer translates of one wavelet fall midway between the integer translates of the other wavelet. In this way, framelet transform are having more wavelets than necessary which further gives a closer spacing between adjacent wavelets within the same scale.
- Framelet transform allows for lesser rectangular artifacts and has near shift-invariance behavior due to the dense time-scale plane when compared with the case of non-oversampled filter banks used in the wavelet related transform.

3.1. Perfect Reconstruction Conditions

Now, the perfect reconstruction conditions for the framelet transform must be studied. Since, three filters h_0, h_1 and h_2 are used for constructing $\phi(t)$, $\psi_1(t)$ and $\psi_2(t)$ respectively. Therefore, framelet transform is based on the three band filter bank. This filter bank is defined in the terms of its polyphase components as

$$H_i(z) = H_{i,0}(z^2) + \frac{1}{z}H_{i,1}(z^2),\ i = 0, 1, 2 \tag{5}$$

where

$$H_{i,0}(z) = \sum_n h_i(2n)z^{-n},\ \ H_{i,1}(z) = \sum_n h_i(2n-1)z^{-n} \tag{6}$$

Using Eqns. 5 and 6, the polyphase analysis matrix is defined as

$$H(z) = \begin{bmatrix} H_{0,0}(z) & H_{1,0}(z) & H_{2,0}(z) \\ H_{0,1}(z) & H_{1,1}(z) & H_{2,1}(z) \end{bmatrix} \tag{7}$$

Now, if a signal $X(z)$ is defined in terms of its polyphase components then

$$X(z) = [X_0(z)\ \ X_1(z)]^T \tag{8}$$

where $X_0(z)$ and $X_1(z)$ are defined in terms of time domain signal $x(n)$ as follows

$$X_i(z) = \sum_n x(2n - i)z^{-n},\ i = 1, 2. \tag{9}$$

To develop the perfect reconstruction conditions, the standard multirate identities are used to write $Y(z)$ in terms of $X(z)$.

$$\begin{aligned} Y(z) &= \frac{1}{2}\left[H_0(z)H_0(1/z) + H_1(z)H_1(1/z) + H_2(z)H_2(1/z)\right]X(z) \\ &+\frac{1}{2}\left[H_0(z)H_0(-1/z) + H_1(z)H_1(-1/z) + H_2(z)H_2(-1/z)\right]X(-z) \end{aligned} \tag{10}$$

For perfect reconstruction, $Y(z) = X(z)$, it is necessary that

$$\begin{aligned} H_0(z)H_0(1/z) + H_1(z)H_1(1/z) + H_2(z)H_2(1/z) = 2 \\ H_0(z)H_0(-1/z) + H_1(z)H_1(-1/z) + H_2(z)H_2(-1/z) = 0 \end{aligned} \tag{11}$$

Using Eqns. 5–7, the perfect reconstruction condition (Eqn. 11) reduces to

$$H(z)H^T(1/z) = I \tag{12}$$

The matrix $H(z)$ is said to be a 2×3 lossless system[60]. Once the values of six components $H_{0,0}$, $H_{1,0}$, $H_{2,0}$, $H_{0,1}$, $H_{1,1}$ and $H_{2,1}$ are obtained such that $H(z)$ satisfies Eqn. 12, the filters $h_0(n)$, $h_1(n)$ and $h_2(n)$ are then formed. The efficient way to obtain 2×3 lossless system is to first determine a 3×3 lossless system followed by the deletion of last row. The brief description on the computation of $H(z)$ can be found in [60].

3.2. Multilevel Structure of Framelet Transform

It is evident that in most of wavelet based applications, the multilevel decomposition structure of wavelet transform is used. Therefore, the framelet transform can be used in all those applications instead of wavelet transform with multilevel structure, it can also be obtained by the repeated process as one does with wavelet transform. The above mentioned framelet transform is applied for the first level decomposition. Afterwards, a low-frequency and two high-frequency bands are obtained (see figure 2). This structure can be obtained by decomposing the low-frequency band by 1-level framelet transform which results in the

2-level framelet transform and this process is further continued until a desired level is not achieved (see figure 3 for 2-level framelet transform). The maximum level of framelet transform depends on how many data points are contained in a data set, since there is a down-sampling by 2 from one level to the next one. The number of level, is chosen in such a way that the noise present in the original signal is removed significantly.

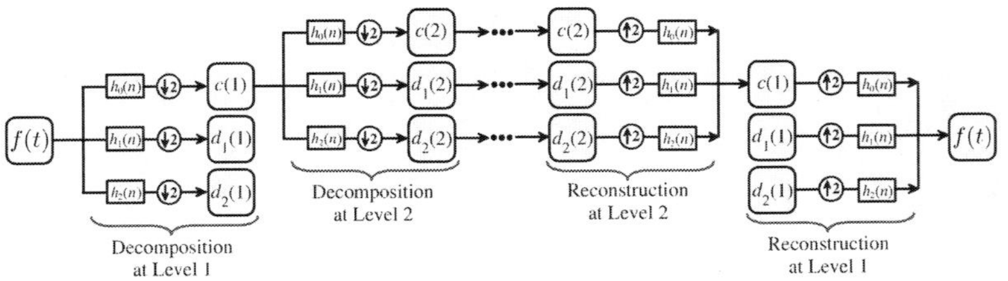

Figure 3. 2-level Framelet Structure of a function $f(t)$: Decomposition and Reconstruction Process.

3.3. Extension to Higher Dimension

Due to the separability of the transform, the framelet transform cab be easily extended to the higher dimension. The separable framelet transform can be obtained by applying one dimension framelet transform along all directions. For instance, if framelet transform in two dimension is considered, the framelet transform is obtained by successive application of one dimension transform along x- and y-axis respectively. Therefore, the whole process is equivalent to two one dimension transforms in series. It is implemented as one dimension row transform followed by a one dimension column transform on the data obtained from the row transform. Since, one scaling and two wavelet functions are used in one dimension transform which further forms the one scaling and eight wavelet functions. These scaling and wavelet functions associated with 2-D framelet transform are obtained by convolving the 1-D filters. Mathematically,

$$\begin{array}{c|ccc} \star & \phi(y) & \psi_1(y) & \psi_2(y) \\ \hline \phi(x) & \phi(x)\star\phi(y) & \phi(x)\star\psi_1(y) & \phi(x)\star\psi_2(y) \\ \psi_1(x) & \psi_1(x)\star\phi(y) & \psi_1(x)\star\psi_1(y) & \psi_1(x)\star\psi_2(y) \\ \psi_2(x) & \psi_2(x)\star\phi(y) & \psi_2(x)\star\psi_1(y) & \psi_2(x)\star\psi_2(y) \end{array} \tag{13}$$

where $\star$ is the conventional convolution operator, $\{\phi(x),\ \psi_1(x),\ \psi_2(x)\}$ and

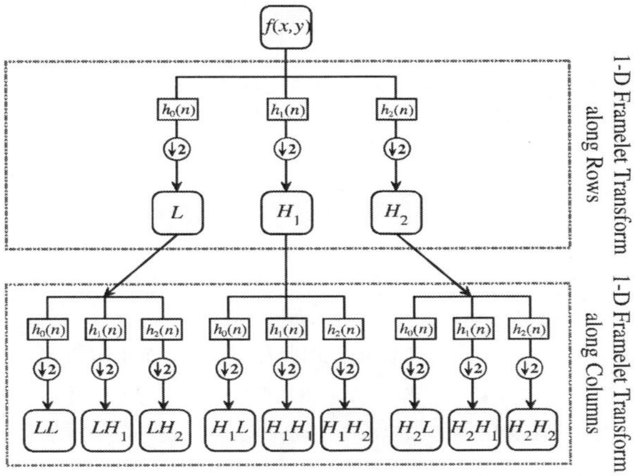

Figure 4. Two Dimensional Framelet Transform Structure of a function $f(x, y)$.

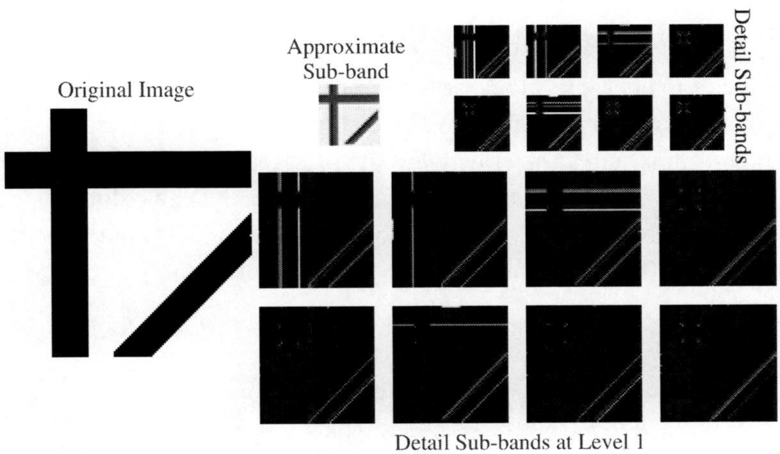

Figure 5. 2-level Framelet Transform of Synthetic Image (Pink colormap is used for better visualization).

$\{\phi(y),\ \psi_1(y),\ \psi_2(y)\}$ are the basis function of 1-D framelet transform along $x-$ and $y-$ direction respectively. The above mentioned Eqn. 13 gives the scaling and wavelet functions used in 2-D framelet transform as basis function.

These basis functions are

2-D Scaling Function	2-D Wavelet Function	
$\psi(x,y)=\psi(x)\star\psi(y)$	$\psi_1(x,y)=\phi(x)\star\psi_1(y)$	$\psi_2(x,y)=\phi(x)\star\psi_2(y)$
	$\psi_3(x,y)=\psi_1(x)\star\phi(y)$	$\psi_4(x,y)=\psi_1(x)\star\psi_1(y)$
	$\psi_5(x,y)=\psi_1(x)\star\psi_2(y)$	$\psi_6(x,y)=\psi_2(x)\star\phi(y)$
	$\psi_7(x,y)=\psi_2(x)\star\psi_1(y)$	$\psi_8(x,y)=\psi_2(x)\star\psi_2(y)$

(14)

The forward framelet transform procedure is shown in figure 4. After applying 1-D transform along $x-$axis, one low-frequency band (L) and two high frequency bands (H_1 and H_2) are obtained. Now, 1-D transform is again applied to these frequency bands along $y-$ axis to finally get one low-frequency (LL) and eight high-frequency bands ($LH_1, LH_2, H_1L, H_1H_1, H_1H_2, H_2L, H_2H_1$ and H_2H_2). Figure 5 shows an example of the 2-level 2-D framelet transform of a synthetic image.

3.4. Block Artifacts Analysis of Framelet Transform

In order to check the block artifacts produced by any transform, the simplest way is to project an image onto the scaling and wavelet spaces at a single level. A transform is said to be effective if the projected image has minimal block artifacts. In figure 6, a synthetic line image is projected and reconstructed from different levels of 4 scale decomposition. From figure, it is clear that the framelet transform suffers from fewer block artifacts when compared to wavelet transform.

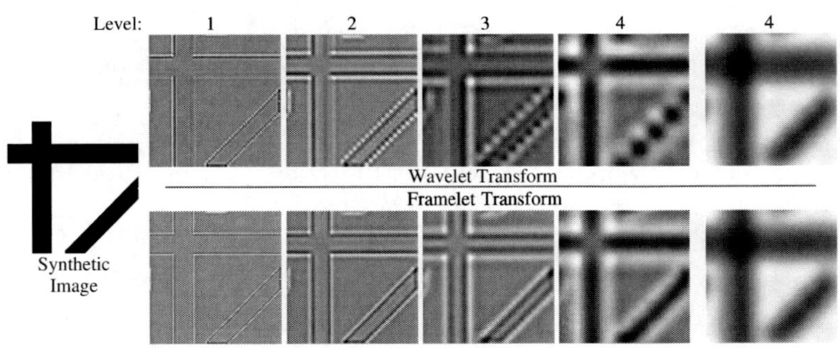

Figure 6. Block artifacts analysis: reconstruction of a synthetic image from the coefficients at single level.

4. Proposed Fusion Technique

The aim of this paper is to ensure the transferability of the most relevant information found in source images into a new composite image with the least amount of required processing. A new efficient framework that combines the advantages of framelet transform and human visual system is developed. Before going to the proposed framework, first the used features extraction models are described.

4.1. Feature Extraction Models

Feature extraction research offers the mathematical models about how to simplify the amount of resources required to describe a large set of data accurately. A lot of work has been explored to address this and then applying it to various image processing applications. The illustrations of the used feature extraction models are as follows.

4.1.1. Local Visibility of an Image

Being inspired from the human visual system, Visibility of an image was introduced by Huang [62] and further extended by Li [63]. Mathematically, visibility of an image (F) is given by:

$$V(F) = \frac{1}{m \times n} \sum_{x=1}^{m} \sum_{y=1}^{n} \left(\frac{1}{\mu_F}\right)^{\alpha} \cdot \frac{|F(x,y) - \mu_F|}{\mu_F} \tag{15}$$

where $m \times n$ is the total number of pixels, μ_F is the mean gray value of the image (F) and α is a visual constant ranging from 0.6 to 0.7. In order to represent the clarity of a pixel, the aforementioned definition of visibility is operated locally to get local visibility (V_L) of the image. Mathematically, V_L is defined as

$$V_L^F(x,y) = \begin{cases} \frac{1}{S_p \times S_p} \sum\limits_{i=x-\frac{S_p}{2}}^{x+\frac{S_p}{2}} \sum\limits_{j=y-\frac{S_p}{2}}^{y+\frac{S_p}{2}} \left(\frac{1}{\widehat{F}(x,y)}\right)^{\alpha} \cdot \frac{|F(x+i,y+j) - \widehat{F}(x,y)|}{\widehat{F}(x,y)}, & \widehat{F}(x,y) \neq 0 \\ F(x,y), & \text{otherwise} \end{cases} \tag{16}$$

where $S_p \times S_p$ is the size of the neighborhood window centered at (x, y) and $\widehat{F}(x,y) = \frac{1}{S_p \times S_p} \sum\limits_{i=x-\frac{S_p}{2}}^{x+\frac{S_p}{2}} \sum\limits_{j=y-\frac{S_p}{2}}^{y+\frac{S_p}{2}} F(i,j)$ is the mean intensity value of F in the neighborhood window.

The significance of local visibility in image fusion is first identified from extensive experiments. For this purpose, the variation of local visibility is explored with respect to the blurriness. The basic idea is to apply average & median filtering and Gaussian blurring on the cameraman image to introduced blurring followed by the local visibility calculation. In figure 7, the local visibility is

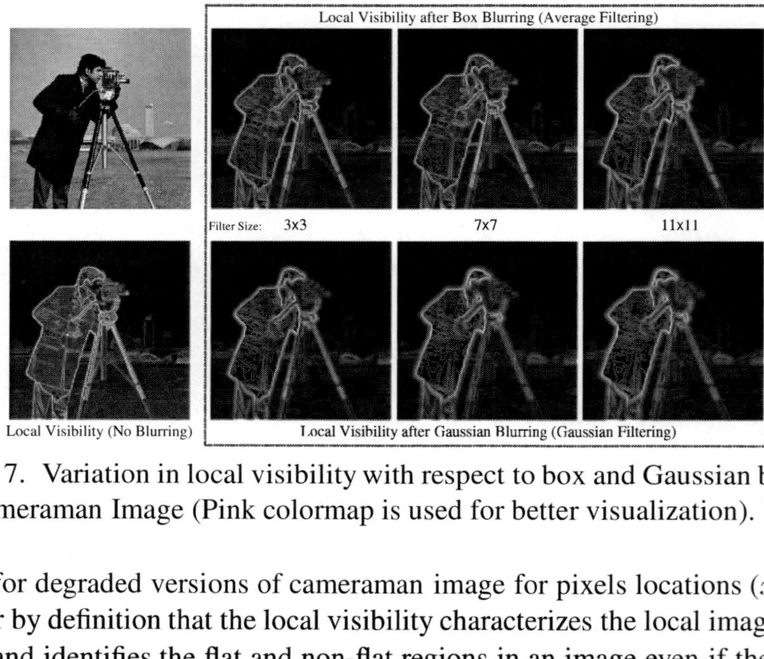

Figure 7. Variation in local visibility with respect to box and Gaussian blurring for Cameraman Image (Pink colormap is used for better visualization).

given for degraded versions of cameraman image for pixels locations (x, y). It is clear by definition that the local visibility characterizes the local image properties and identifies the flat and non-flat regions in an image even if the image is effected by the blurring (box or gaussian blurring). Ideally, the higher values indicates the flat regions whereas lower values indicates non-flat regions.

4.1.2. Smallest Univalue Segment Assimilating Nucleus (SUSAN) Feature Extractor

The Smallest Univalue Segment Assimilating Nucleus (SUSAN) feature extraction algorithm was proposed by Smith *et al.* [64] in 1997. The obtained features are usually represented by the texture information (edges and corners) in one and two-dimensions. Since the demonstration of the SUSAN, different applications have been developed such as video-encoding artefact removal, 3D mesh denoising, feature extraction etc. The basic principle of the SUSAN algorithm is to associate each image pixel with its local area of similar intensity. Unlike other existing feature extractor which rely on derivative (first) of the image, SUSAN extractor relies on local binarization of gray-values. To compute the feature of a pixel (called the "nucleus"), a circular mask around the pixel is considered. By choice of a brightness difference threshold, an area within the mask is selected which consists of pixels similar in brightness to the nucleus. The small local area is called the Univalue Segment Assimilating Nucleus (USAN), which contains the most important information about the structure of the image in the region around the center pixel. To be more precise, let the input image is F and the circular mask has a radius of $|\vec{r}|$, then the simplest USAN has the following form.

$$d(\vec{r}, \vec{r}_0) = \begin{cases} 1, & |F(\vec{r}) - F(\vec{r}_0)| \leq T \\ 0, & |F(\vec{r}) - F(\vec{r}_0)| > T \end{cases} \tag{17}$$

where $\vec{r}_0$ and $\vec{r}$ are the position of the central pixel and any other pixels within the mask, respectively, $F(\vec{r})$ is the intensity at $\vec{r}$ and T is the brightness difference threshold. The feature response is calculated as

$$FR(\vec{r}_0) = \begin{cases} \mathcal{T} - n(\vec{r}_0), & n(\vec{r}_0) < \mathcal{T} \\ 0, & \text{otherwise} \end{cases} \tag{18}$$

where $n(\vec{r}_0)$ is the number of pixels belonging to the USAN i.e.

$$n(\vec{r}_0) = \sum_{\vec{r}} d(\vec{r}, \vec{r}_0) \tag{19}$$

and $\mathcal{T}$ is a geometric threshold, which is given as $\mathcal{T} = \frac{3n_{max}}{4}$, where n_{max} is the maximum value of n. A single fixed value of $\mathcal{T}$ can be found by calculating the mean expectation of the edge response in the presence of noise.

In the SUSAN feature detector, T usually determines the minimum contrast of feature to be detected as well as the maximum amount of noise to be ignored. Therefore, sometimes the extracted features become sensitive to the choice of T. To make feature extraction less sensitive to T, a USAN function which takes into account not only the degrees of similarity in brightness but also the distance between pixels as

$$d(\vec{r}, \vec{r}_0) = \exp\left[\frac{-(\vec{r} - \vec{r}_0)^2}{2\eta^2}\right] \exp\left[-\left(\frac{F(\vec{r}) - F(\vec{r}_0)}{T}\right)^6\right] \tag{20}$$

where η is a distance scaling factor. The SUSAN edge position theoretically coincides with the zero-crossing of the second derivative of the image function

[64]. Since edges and corners do not directly depend on any derivatives and maximum gradient direction, the effect of noise on edge localization is reduced considerably.

4.2. Proposed Multimodal Medical Image Fusion Framework

In this section, some of the motivating factors in the design of our approach to multimodal medical image fusion are discussed. For our convenience, only two source images are considered in our experiment, let they be F_1 and F_2. The method can of course be easily extended to more than two images. It is assumed here that source images have been well registered. The general procedure of the proposed framework is depicted in figure 8 and can be summarized as follows:

1. Perform ℓ-level framelet transform on source images to obtain low and high-frequency bands at each level, which are denoted by $f^{\theta}_{l,1}$ and $f^{\theta}_{l,2}$ respectively, where $l \in [1, \ell]$ is the level of decomposition and $\theta \in \{LL, LH_1,\ LH_2, H_1L, H_1H_1, H_1H_2,\ H_2L,\ H_2H_1, H_2H_2\}$ represents the orientation of the frequency bands..

2. *Fusion of Low-frequency Bands:* Low-frequency bands obtained by the framelet transform are the approximate version of source images and usually include average gray information. The simplest way is to use the conventional averaging or weighted average methods to produce the composite bands. However, it cannot give the fused low-frequency component of high quality for medical image because it leads to the reduced contrast in the fused images. Therefore, a new criterion is proposed here based on local visibility of the image. For this purpose, the local visibility in the framelet domain is chosen as the measurement. The complete process is described as follows.

   ► Calculate the local visibility inside the $S_p \times S_p$ neighborhood (say $\mathcal{N}$) centering the current coefficient in the low-frequency band, which is

$$V^{f^{LL}_{\ell,1}}(x,y) = V\left(f^{LL}_{\ell,1}(\mathcal{N})\right) \tag{21}$$

$$V^{f^{LL}_{\ell,2}}(x,y) = V\left(f^{LL}_{\ell,2}(\mathcal{N})\right) \tag{22}$$

   where (x, y) is the current coefficient position and $\mathcal{N}$ is the $S_p \times S_p$ neighborhood centering at (x, y).

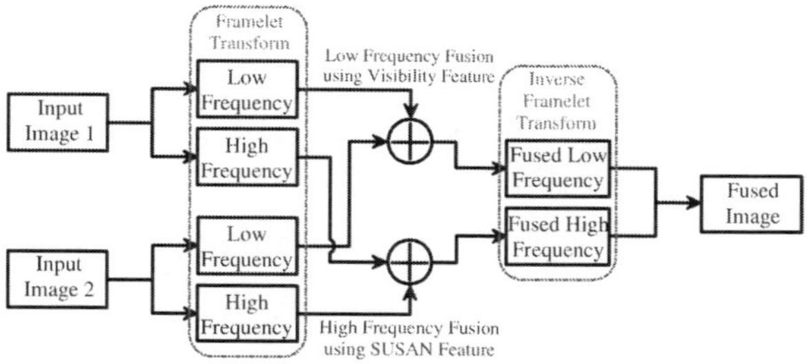

Figure 8. Block Diagram of Proposed Image Fusion Framework.

► Fuse the low frequency bands as

$$f_{\ell,fused}^{LL}(x,y)=\begin{cases} f_{\ell,1}^{LL}(x,y), \text{if } V^{f_{\ell,1}^{LL}}(x,y) \geq V^{f_{\ell,2}^{LL}}(x,y) \\ f_{\ell,2}^{LL}(x,y), \text{if } V^{f_{\ell,1}^{LL}}(x,y) < V^{f_{\ell,2}^{LL}}(x,y) \end{cases} \tag{23}$$

3. *Fusion of High-frequency Bands:* High-frequency bands obtained by the framelet transform usually include edges and corners in various directions. The simplest way is to use the maximum selection method to produce the composite bands. However, this method is not appropriate for medical images since it discards some edges and corners due to maximum selection. Therefore, a new criterion is proposed here based on human visual system. For this purpose, the most prominent edges and corners are identified according to HVS and then selection and averaging is performed. The whole process is described as follows.

► First, the feature is extracted from high-frequency bands at each scale and orientation using SUSAN feature extractor (Eqns. 17–20), denoted by $FR_{f_{l,i}^{\theta}}$, where $i = 1,2$ is the number of image and $\theta \in \{LH_1, LH_2, H_1L, H_1H_1, H_1H_2, H_2L, H_2H_1, H_2H_2\}$.

► Fuse the high-frequency bands as follows.

$$f_{l,fused}^{\theta}(x,y) = \begin{cases} f_{l,1}^{\theta}(x,y), & \text{if } FR^{f_{\ell,1}^{LL}}(x,y) < FR^{f_{\ell,2}^{LL}}(x,y) \\ f_{l,2}^{\theta}(x,y), & \text{if } FR^{f_{\ell,1}^{LL}}(x,y) > FR^{f_{\ell,2}^{LL}}(x,y) \\ \dfrac{f_{l,1}^{\theta}(x,y)+f_{l,1}^{\theta}(x,y)}{2}, & \text{if } FR^{f_{\ell,1}^{LL}}(x,y) = FR^{f_{\ell,2}^{LL}}(x,y) \end{cases} \tag{24}$$

4. Perform ℓ-level framelet transform on fused low and high-frequency bands at each level, to get fused image (F).

5. Results and Discussions

Some general requirements for fusion algorithm are: (1) it should be able to extract complimentary features from input images, (2) it must not introduce artifacts or inconsistencies according to Human Visual System and (3) it should be robust and reliable. Generally, these requirements are often very difficult to achieve. One of the most critical problems is that there is a lack of reliable and efficient methods to validate fusion algorithms. The best method to validate the fusion algorithm is that some human observers are asked to view a series of fused images and rate them. These tests are typically accurate if performed correctly but they are inconvenient, expensive and time consuming. Hence, there is a need to create an evaluation system. Therefore, first an evaluation index system is established to evaluate the proposed fusion algorithm. These indices are determined according to the statistical parameters. This evaluation index system includes mean, standard deviation, entropy, spatial frequency, mutual information, normalized singular value similarity, structural similarity and edge based similarity. Among these mean, standard deviation, entropy and spatial frequency reflect spatial details information whereas mutual information, normalized singular value similarity, structural similarity and edge based similarity reflect spectral information contained in the fused image. Mathematical definitions of these indices are given below.

5.1. Evaluation Index System

1. *Mean and Standard Deviation:* In statistical theory, mean and standard deviation are defined as follows:

$$\begin{aligned} \hat{\mu} &= \frac{1}{MN}\sum_{i=1}^{M}\sum_{j=1}^{N} x_{i,j}, \\ \hat{\sigma}^2 &= \frac{1}{(M-1)\,(N-1)}\sum_{i=1}^{M}\sum_{j=1}^{N}(x_{i,j}-\hat{\mu})^2 \end{aligned} \tag{14}$$

   where MN is the total number of pixels in the image and $x_{i,j}$ is the value of the ij^{th} pixel.

2. *Entropy:* Entropy is the measure of information quantity contained in an image. If the value of entropy becomes higher after fusion then the

information quality will increase. Mathematically, entropy is defined as:

$$E = -\sum_{i=1}^{M}\sum_{j=1}^{N} p(x_{i,j}) \ln p(x_{i,j}) \tag{15}$$

where $p(x_{i,j})$ is the probability of the occurrence of $x_{i,j}$.

3. *Spatial frequency:* Spatial Frequency (SF) measures the overall activity level in an image. If the value of SF becomes higher after fusion then the activity level will increase. Mathematically, the spatial frequency is defined as:

$$SF = \sqrt{RF^2 + CF^2} \tag{16}$$

where RF and CF are the row and column frequencies and are defined as:

$$RF = \sqrt{\frac{1}{MN}\sum_{i=1}^{M_1}\sum_{j=2}^{N_1}[x_{i,j} - x_{i,j-1}]^2} \tag{17}$$

$$CF = \sqrt{\frac{1}{MN}\sum_{j=1}^{N_1}\sum_{i=2}^{M_1}[x_{i,j} - x_{i-1,j}]^2} \tag{18}$$

4. *Mutual Information:* Mutual Information (MI) is the measure of information shared by two images. If the value of MI becomes higher after fusion then the information quality will increase. Mathematically, MI is defined as:

$$MI = \sum_{i=1}^{L}\sum_{j=1}^{L} h_{i,j}^{x,y} \log_2 \frac{h_{i,j}^{x,y}}{h_{i,j}^{x}\ h_{i,j}^{y}} \tag{19}$$

where $h^{x,y}$ is the normalized joint grey-level histogram of images x and y, h^x, h^y are the normalized marginal histograms of the two images and L is the number of gray-levels. Based on the above definition, the quality of the fused image with respect to input images A and B can be expressed as

$$Q_{MI} = 2\left[\frac{MI(A,F)}{H(A)+H(F)} + \frac{MI(B,F)}{H(B)+H(F)}\right] \tag{20}$$

where $H(A)$, $H(B)$ and $H(F)$ is the marginal entropy of images A, B and F respectively. The higher the value of Q_{MI}, the better the fused image is.

5. *Structural Similarity:* Structural similarity (SSIM) is designed by modeling any image distortion as the combination of loss of correlation, radiometric distortion and contrast distortion. SSIM is defined as:

$$SSIM = \frac{\sigma_{xy}}{\sigma_x\,\sigma_y}\,\frac{2\mu_x\,\mu_y}{\mu_x^2+\mu_y^2}\,\frac{2\sigma_x\,\sigma_y}{\sigma_x^2+\sigma_y^2} \tag{21}$$

where μ_x, μ_y are mean intensity and σ_x, σ_y, σ_{xy} are the standard deviation. In equation 22, first term is the correlation coefficient between x and y. The second term measures how close the mean grey level is, third term measures the similarity in contrast of x and y. Based on the definition of SSIM, a new way to use SSIM for the image fusion assessment is defined as

$$Q_S = \begin{cases} \lambda(w)SSIM(A,F|w) + (1-\lambda(w))SSIM(B,F|w), \\ \qquad\qquad\qquad\qquad \text{if } SSIM(A,B|w) \geq 0.75 \\ \max\left[SSIM(A,F|w), SSIM(B,F|w)\right], \\ \qquad\qquad\qquad\qquad \text{if } SSIM(A,B|w) < 0.75 \end{cases} \tag{22}$$

where w is a sliding window of size 3×3, which moves pixel by pixel from the top-left to the bottom-right corner and $\lambda(w)$ is the local weight obtained from the local image salience. The higher the value of Q_S, the better the fused image is.

6. *Edge Based Similarity Measure*: The edge based similarity measure gives the similarity between the edges transferred in the fusion process. Mathematically, $Q^{AB/F}$ is defined as

$$Q^{AB/F} = \frac{\sum\limits_{i=1}^{M}\sum\limits_{j=1}^{N}\left[Q_{i,j}^{AF}\,w_{i,j}^{x} + Q_{i,j}^{BF}\,w_{i,j}^{y}\right]}{\sum\limits_{i=1}^{M}\sum\limits_{j=1}^{N}\left[w_{i,j}^{x} + w_{i,j}^{y}\right]} \tag{23}$$

where A, B and F represent the input and fused images respectively. The definition of Q^{AF} and Q^{BF} are same and given as

$$Q_{i,j}^{AF} = Q_{g,\,i,j}^{AF}\,Q_{\alpha,\,i,j}^{AF}, \quad Q_{i,j}^{BF} = Q_{g,\,i,j}^{BF}\,Q_{\alpha,\,i,j}^{BF} \tag{24}$$

where $Q_g^{\star F}$ and $Q_\alpha^{\star F}$ are the edge strength and orientation preservation values at location (i,j) respectively for images A and B. The dynamic range for $Q^{AB/F}$ is [0,1] and it should be as close to 1 as possible for better fusion.

Among these mean, standard deviation, entropy and spatial frequency reflect spatial details information whereas mutual information similarity, structural similarity and edge based similarity reflect spectral information contained in the fused image. The metrics Q_{MI}, Q_S and $Q^{AB/F}$ utilizes all input and fused image to evaluate the performance, however, others utilizes only fused images.

5.2. Experiments and Results

In medical diagnostics, the commonly used medical imaging modalities are computed tomography (CT) and nuclear magnetic resonance (NMR) imaging. Both of these imaging modalities are complementary in nature. CT images are sensitive to bone and hard tissues while MR images are more informative about soft tissues. Fusion of these two will provide a single image, which will assist the physician to localize abnormalities and to do a better diagnosis.

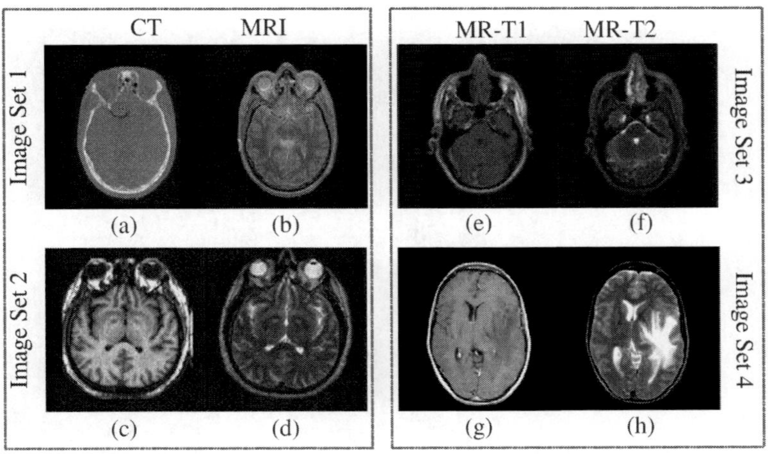

Figure 9. Multimodal medical image sets.

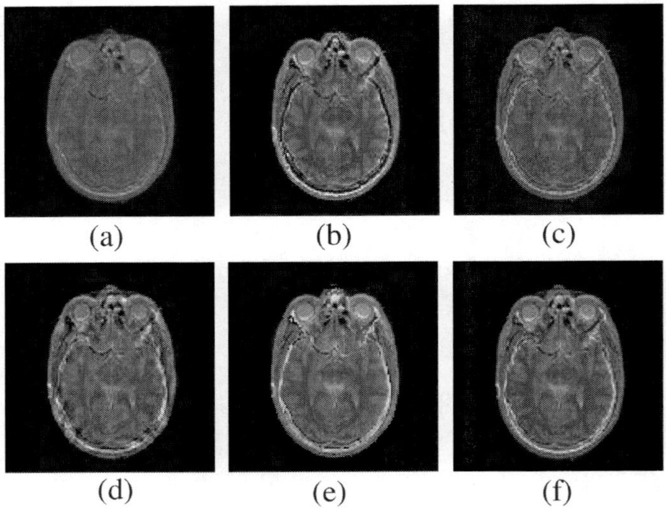

Figure 10. Results for data set 1: Fused image for a) PCA method b) contrast pyramid c) gradient pyramid d) wavelet method e) morphological wavelet method f) proposed method.

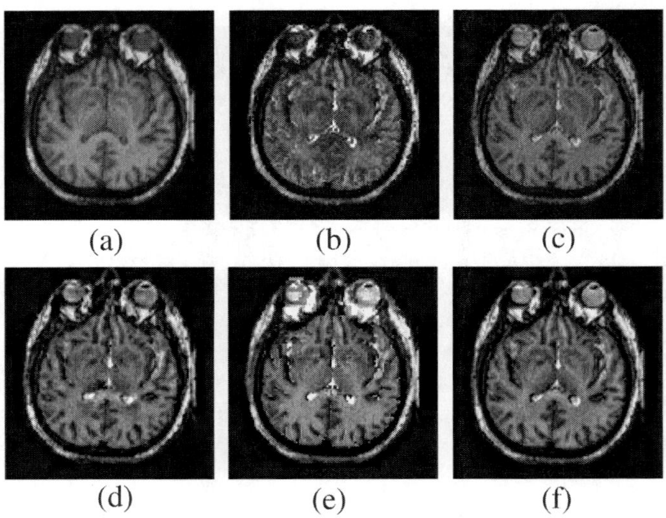

Figure 11. Results for data set 2: Fused image for a) PCA method b) contrast pyramid c) gradient pyramid d) wavelet method e) morphological wavelet method f) proposed method.

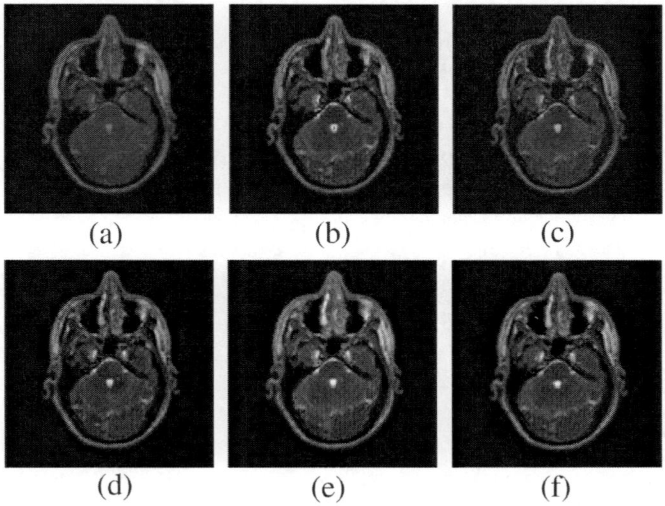

Figure 12. Results for data set 3: Fused image for a) PCA method b) contrast pyramid c) gradient pyramid d) wavelet method e) morphological wavelet method f) proposed method.

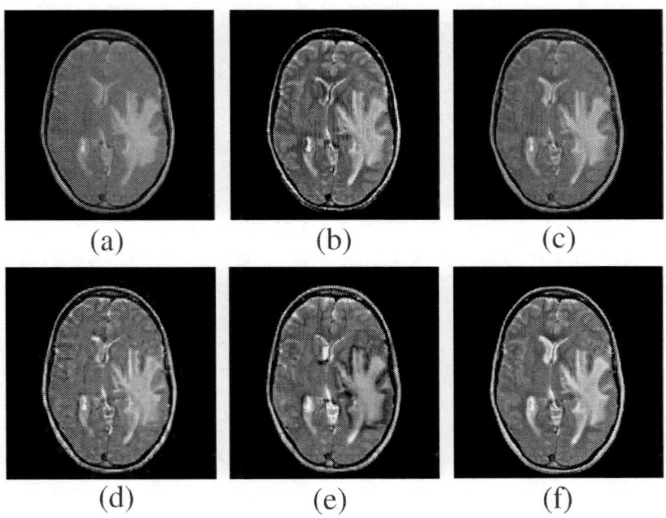

Figure 13. Results for data set 4: Fused image for a) PCA method b) contrast pyramid c) gradient pyramid d) wavelet method e) morphological wavelet method f) proposed method.

Table 2. Evaluation Indices for Fused Medical Images

Images	Indices	PCA	Contrast [18]	Gradient [19]	Wavelet [21]	Morphological [22]	Proposed
Data Set 1	Mean	47.1462	48.4901	48.7045	47.2150	49.8023	47.1154
	St.D.	50.6755	57.0108	51.2016	54.0375	59.3273	54.8656
	Entropy	5.0798	5.6955	5.9718	5.8247	5.6771	5.7264
	SF	6.4346	8.3020	7.9483	8.2611	7.9368	8.1442
	Q_{MI}	3.2783	3.5385	3.6809	3.1846	2.9278	3.1814
	Q_S	0.7961	0.9108	0.7916	0.8096	0.7670	0.8226
	$Q^{AB/F}$	0.3814	0.5621	0.4992	0.4705	0.5611	0.5683
Data Set 2	Mean	63.6088	56.0327	59.9091	58.3433	64.1198	58.2527
	St.D.	55.2365	54.9344	49.9491	56.1647	65.7601	59.2071
	Entropy	6.6012	6.7343	6.7807	6.8588	6.7590	6.8349
	SF	9.4115	10.1713	10.1400	10.5434	10.0470	10.4545
	Q_{MI}	3.8661	3.0930	3.4319	3.5919	3.5052	3.8011
	Q_S	0.9217	0.6113	0.7717	0.7367	0.7033	0.7763
	$Q^{AB/F}$	0.5591	0.3795	0.4946	0.4619	0.4900	0.5439
Data Set 3	Mean	28.6358	29.3533	29.0560	28.6402	32.7299	28.1963
	St.D.	29.0901	33.6854	29.6112	33.7081	39.7143	35.3860
	Entropy	4.7567	5.2728	5.3582	5.3257	5.4176	5.3667
	SF	6.6341	7.7083	7.6069	7.9243	7.8299	7.8090
	Q_{MI}	3.9423	3.4623	3.2840	3.7273	3.2798	3.9866
	Q_S	0.8883	0.8655	0.8512	0.8196	0.8105	0.8233
	$Q^{AB/F}$	0.5559	0.6015	0.6460	0.6191	0.6452	0.6632
Data Set 4	Mean	51.3621	49.3053	51.4831	52.2611	48.3948	52.5929
	St.D.	61.3152	64.3439	62.0742	64.8365	62.6458	67.2087
	Entropy	4.4823	4.4506	4.8556	4.6912	4.4955	4.3012
	SF	5.4963	6.9100	6.2114	6.7521	6.9078	6.7992
	Q_{MI}	3.6664	3.4432	3.4061	3.1602	3.3239	3.2702
	Q_S	0.7889	0.8488	0.7937	0.7587	0.7831	0.8314
	$Q^{AB/F}$	0.4534	0.4634	0.5767	0.5484	0.5584	0.6297

The proposed multimodal medical image fusion approach is evaluated over four different sets of multimodal images of size 256×256 (see figure 9). Among these sets of medical images, the first two sets of medical images are normal CT and MRI image whereas the other two sets are T1- and T2-weighted MR images. Without loss of generality, it is assumed that the corresponding pixels of the two input images have been perfectly co-aligned. It can be seen that due to various imaging principles and environments, the source images with different modality contain complementary information, which are fused to get a single image having better localization of abnormalities.

For all these image sets, results of proposed fusion framework are compared with the traditional PCA (MS rule), gradient pyramid [19], contrast pyramid [18], wavelet [21] and morphological wavelet [22] based methods. The comparison of statistical parameters for fused images according to different fusion algorithms are shown in table 2 and visually in figure 10-13. From figures, it is clear that the proposed algorithms not only preserve spectral information but also improve the spatial detail information than the existing algorithms, which can easily be observed by the obtained maximum values of evaluation indices (table 2). The PCA algorithm gives baseline results. Except one or two cases, these methods give poor results relative to other algorithms. This was expected because this method has no scale selectivity. This limitation is rectified in pyramid and multiresolution based algorithms but on the cost of quality i.e. the contrast of the fuse image is reduced which is greater in pyramid based algorithms and comparatively less in multiresolution based algorithms. Among multiresolution based algorithms, the proposed algorithm based on framelet transform performs better. The main reason behind the better performance is the used HVS models and main properties of framelet transform such as symmetry, simple sampling and large vanishing moments by which smoother scaling and more informative wavelet coefficients are produced compared to other multiresolution methods.

Conclusion

In this paper, a novel multimodality image fusion algorithm based on framelet transform is proposed. Considering the feature extraction models, two different fusion rules are proposed by which more information can be preserved in the fused image with improved quality. The used features include visibility and SUSAN feature extractor and are adopted as the fusion measurement for coefficients combination in low- and high-frequency bands. In our experiment, four groups of CT/MRI image are fused using conventional fusion algorithms and the proposed framelet-based algorithm. The visual and statistical comparisons demonstrate that the proposed algorithm better preserved the image details and significantly improved the image visual effect than the other fusion methods with very less information distortion.

References

[1] F. Maes, D. Vandermeulen, and P. Suetens, "Medical image registration using mutual information," in Proceedings of *IEEE*, vol. 91, no. 10, 2003, pp. 1699–1721.

[2] M. Aguilar, A.L. Garrett, "Neuro-physiologically motivated sensor fusion for visualization and characterization of medical imagery," in Proceeding of *International Conference on Information Fusion*, Montreal, QC, Canada, 2001.

[3] A.P. James and B.V. Dasarathy, "Medical image fusion: A survey of the state of the art," *Information Fusion*, vol. 19, 2014, pp. 4–19.

[4] S.G. Nikolov, P.R. Hill, D.R. Bull and C.N. Canagarajah, "Wavelets for image fusion," in: A. Petrosian, F. Meyer (Eds.), *Wavelets in Signal and Image Analysis, Computational Imaging and Vision Series*, Kluwer Academic Publishers, Dordrecht, The Netherlands, 2001, pp. 213-244.

[5] O. Rockinger and T. Fechner, "Pixel level fusion: the case of image sequences," *Proceedings of the SPIE*, vol. 3374, 1998, pp. 378–388.

[6] Y. Nakamoto, K. Tamai, T. Saga, T. Higashi, T. Hara, T. Suga, T. Koyama and K. Togashi, "Clinical value of image fusion from MR and PET in patients with head and neck Cancer," *Molecular Imaging and Biology*, vol. 11, no. 1, 2009, pp. 46–53.

[7] F.L. Giesel, A. Mehndiratta, J. Locklin, M.J. McAuliffe, S. White, P.L. Choyke, M.V. Knopp, B.J. Wood, U. Haberkorn and H.V. Tengg-Kobligk, "Image fusion using CT, MRI and PET for treatment planning, navigation and follow up in percutaneous RFA," *Experimental Oncology*, vol. 31, no. 2, 2009, pp. 106–114.

[8] N. Kannathal, U.R. Acharya, E.Y.K. Ng, S.M. Krishnan, L.C. Min and S. Laxminarayan, "Cardiac health diagnosis using data fusion of cardiovascular and haemodynamic signals," *Computer Methods and Programs in Biomedicine*, vol. 82, no. 2, 2006, pp. 87–96.

[9] A.I. Hernandez, G. Carrault, F. Mora, L. Thoraval, G. Passariello and J.M. Schleich, "Multisensor fusion for atrial and ventricular activity detection in coronary care monitoring," *IEEE Transactions on Biomedical Engineering*, vol. 46, no. 10, 1999, pp. 1186–1190.

[10] F. Lindseth, S. Ommedal, J. Bang, G. Unsgard and T.A.N. Hernes, "Image fusion of ultrasound and MRI as an aid for assessing anatomical shifts and improving overview and interpretation in ultrasound-guided neurosurgery," *International Congress Series*, vol. 1230, 2001, pp. 254–260.

[11] G.M. Rojas, U. Raff, J.C. Quintana, I. Huete and M. Hutchinson, "Image fusion in neuroradiology: three clinical examples including MRI of Parkinson disease," *Computerized Medical Imaging and Graphics*, vol. 31, no. 1, 2007, pp. 17–27.

[12] C.S. Xydeas and V. Petrovic, "Objective Pixel-level Image Fusion Performance Measure," *Procedding of SPIE*, vol. 4051, 2002, pp. 89–98.

[13] A. Cardinali and G.P. Nason, "A Statistical Multiscale Approach to Image Segmentation and Fusion," in *Proceedings of International Conference on Information Fusion*, Philadelphia, PA, USA, 2005, pp. 475–482.

[14] K. Mikoajczyk, J. Owczarczyk and W. Recko, "A test-bed for computer-assisted fusion of multi-modality medical images," *Computer Analysis of Images and Patterns*, Lecture Notes in Computer Science, vol. 719, 1993, pp 664–668.

[15] G. Matsopoulos, S. Marshall and J. Brunt, "Multiresolution morphological fusion of MR and CT images of the human brain," *IEE Proceedings-Vision, Image and Signal Processing*, vol. 141, no. 3, 1994, pp. 137–142.

[16] C. Kok, Y. Hui and T. Nguyen, "Medical image pseudo coloring by wavelet fusion," in *Proceedings of International Conference of the IEEE Engineering in Medicine and Biology Society*, vol. 2, 1996, pp. 648–649.

[17] R. Kapoor, A. Dutta, D. Bagai and T. S. Kamal, "Fusion for registration of medical images-a study," in *Proceedings of Applied Imagery Pattern Recognition Workshop*, 2003, pp. 180–185.

[18] P.J. Burt and R.J. Kolczynski, "Enhanced image capture through fusion," in Proceedings of *International Conference on Computer Vision*, Berlin, Germany, 1993, pp. 173–182.

[19] V.S. Petrovic and C.S. Xydeas, "Gradient-based multiresolution image fusion," *IEEE Transactions on Image Processing*, vol. 13, no. 2, 2004, pp. 228–237.

[20] H. Li, B.S. Manjunath and S.K. Mitra, "Multisensor image fusion using the wavelet transform," *Graphical Models and Image Processing*, vol. 57, no. 3, 1995, pp. 235–245.

[21] Q. Guihong, Z. Dali and Y. Pingfan, "Medical image fusion by wavelet transform modulus maxima," *Optics Express*, vol. 9, 2001, pp. 184–190.

[22] I. De and B. Chanda, "A simple and efficient algorithm for multifocus image fusion using morphological wavelets", *Signal Processing*, vol. 86, 2006, pp. 924–936.

[23] G. Bhatnagar and Q.M.J. Wu, "An Image Fusion Framework Based on Human Visual System in Framelet Domain," *International Journal of Wavelets, Multiresolution and Information Processing*, vol. 10, no. 1, 2012, pp. 1250002-1–30.

[24] G. Bhatnagar, Q.M.J. Wu and Z. Liu, "Human visual system inspired multi-modal medical image fusion framework," *Expert Systems with Applications*, vol. 40, no. 5, 2013, pp. 1708–1720.

[25] F. Nencini, A. Garzelli, S. Baronti and L. Alparone, "Remote sensing image fusion using the curvelet transform," *Information Fusion*, vol. 8, no. 2, 2007, pp. 143–156.

[26] L. Yang, B. Guo and W. Ni, "Multimodality medical image fusion based on multiscale geometric analysis of contourlet transform," *Neurocomputing*, vol. 72, no. 13, 2008, pp. 203–211.

[27] Q. Zhang and B.L. Guo, "Multi-focus image fusion using the nonsubsampled contourlet transform," *Signal Processing*, vol. 89, no. 7, 2009, pp. 1334–1346.

[28] G. Bhatnagar, Q.M.J. Wu and Z. Liu, "Directive Contrast Based Multimodal Medical Image Fusion in NSCT Domain," *IEEE Transactions on Multimedia*, vol. 15, no. 5, 2013, pp. 1014–1024.

[29] S. Garg, K. U. Kiran, R. Mohan and U. Tiwary, "Multilevel medical image fusion using segmented image by level set evolution with region competition," in Proceedings of *International Conference of the Engineering in Medicine and Biology Society*, 2006, pp. 7680–7683.

[30] L. Bin, T. Lianfang, K. Yuanyuan and Y. Xia, "Parallel multimodal medical image fusion in 3D conformal radiotherapy treatment planning," in Proceedings of *International Conference on Bioinformatics and Biomedical Engineering*, 2008, pp. 2600–2604.

[31] M. Ciampi, "Medical image fusion for color visualization via 3D RDWT," in Proceedings of *IEEE International Conference on Information Technology and Applications in Biomedicine*, 2010, pp. 1–6.

[32] S.-H. Lai and M. Fang, "Adaptive medical image visualization based on hierarchical neural networks and intelligent decision fusion," in Proceedings of *IEEE Signal Processing Society Workshop on Neural Networks for Signal Processing VIII*, 1998, pp. 438–447.

[33] G.L. Rogova and P.C. Stomper, "Information fusion approach to microcalcification characterization," *Information Fusion*, vol. 3, no. 2, 2002, pp. 91–102.

[34] Z. Wang and Y. Ma, "Medical image fusion using m-PCNN," *Information Fusion*, vol. 9, no. 2, 2008, pp. 176–185.

[35] J. Teng, S. Wang, J. Zhang and X. Wang, "Neuro-fuzzy logic based fusion algorithm of medical images," in Proceedings of *International Congress on Image and Signal Processing*, vol. 4, 2010, pp. 1552–1556.

[36] Y. Wu, C. Wang, S.C. Ng, A. Madabhushi and Y. Zhong, "Breast cancer diagnosis using neural-based linear fusion strategies," in *Proceedings*

of International Conference on Neural Information Processing, 2006, pp. 165–175.

[37] D. Lederman, B. Zheng, X. Wang, X.H. Wang and D. Gur, "Improving breast cancer risk stratification using resonance-frequency electrical impedance spectroscopy through fusion of multiple classifiers," *Annals of Biomedical Engineering*, vol. 39, no. 3, 2011, pp. 931–945.

[38] M.S.B. Sehgal, I. Gondal and L. Dooley, "Support vector machine and generalized regression neural network based classification fusion models for cancer diagnosis," in Proceedings of *International Conference on Hybrid Intelligent Systems*, 2004, pp. 49–54.

[39] F. Masulli and S. Mitra, "Natural computing methods in bioinformatics: a survey," *Information Fusion*, vol. 10, no. 3, 2009, pp. 211–216.

[40] V. Barra and J.-Y. Boire, "A general framework for the fusion of anatomical and functional medical images," *NeuroImage*, vol. 13, no. 3, 2001, pp. 410–424.

[41] I. Bloch, O. Colliot, O. Camara and T. Geraud, "Fusion of spatial relationships for guiding recognition, example of brain structure recognition in 3D MRI," *Pattern Recognition Letters*, vol. 26, no. 4, 2005, pp. 449–457.

[42] W. Dou, S. Ruan, Y. Chen, D. Bloyet and J.-M. Constans, "A framework of fuzzy information fusion for the segmentation of brain tumor tissues on MR images," *Image Vision and Computing*, vol. 25, no. 2, 2007, pp. 164–171.

[43] R. Wasserman, R. Acharya, C. Sibata and K. Shin, "A data fusion approach to tumor delineation," in Proceedings of *International Conference on Image Processing*, vol. 2, 995, pp. 476–479.

[44] V. Barra and J.-Y. Boire, "Automatic segmentation of subcortical brain structures in MR images using information fusion," *IEEE Transactions on Medical Imaging*, vol. 20, no. 7, 2001, pp. 549–558.

[45] C.-H. Huang and J.-D. Lee, "Improving MMI with enhanced-FCM for the fusion of brain MR and SPECT images," in Proceedings of *International Conference on Pattern Recognition*, vol. 3, 2004, pp. 562–565.

[46] A. Villeger, L. Ouchchane, J.-J. Lemaire and J.-Y. Boire, "Data fusion and fuzzy spatial relationships for locating deep brain stimulation targets in magnetic resonance images," *Advanced Concepts for Intelligent Vision Systems*, Springer, 2006, pp. 909–919.

[47] W. Dou, S. Ruan, Q. Liao, D. Bloyet, J.-M. Constans and Y. Chen, "Fuzzy information fusion scheme used to segment brain tumor from MR images," *Fuzzy Logic and Applications*, Springer, 2006, pp. 208–215.

[48] P.S. Chavez and A.Y. Kwarteng, "Extracting spectral contrast in Landsat thematic mapper image data using selective principal component analysis," *Photogrammetric Engineering and Remote Sensing*, vol. 55, 1989, pp. 339–348.

[49] N. Al-Azzawi, H. A. M. Sakim, A. W. Abdullah and H. Ibrahim, "Medical image fusion scheme using complex contourlet transform based on PCA," in Proceedings of *International Conference of the IEEE Engineering in Medicine and Biology Society*, 2009, pp. 5813–5816.

[50] C. He, Q. Liu, H. Li and H. Wang, "Multimodal medical image fusion based on IHS and PCA," *Procedia Engineering*, vol. 7, 2010, pp. 280–285.

[51] V.D. Calhoun and T. Adali, "Feature-based fusion of medical imaging data," *IEEE Transactions on Information Technology in Biomedicine*, vol. 13, no. 5, 2009, pp. 711–720.

[52] I. Dimou, G. Manikis and M. Zervakis, "Classifier fusion approaches for diagnostic cancer models," in Proceedings of *International Conference of the IEEE Engineering in Medicine and Biology Society*, 2006, pp. 5334–5337.

[53] M. Raza, I. Gondal, D. Green and R. L. Coppel, "Classifier fusion using dempstershafer theory of evidence to predict breast cancer tumors," in Proceedings of *International technical conference of IEEE Region 10*, 2006, pp. 1–4.

[54] N. Zhang, Q. Liao, S. Ruan, S. Lebonvallet and Y. Zhu, "Multi-kernel SVM based classification for tumor segmentation by fusion of MRI images," in Proceedings of *IEEE International Workshop on Imaging Systems and Techniques*, 2009, pp. 71–75.

[55] M.M. Rahman, B.C. Desai and P. Bhattacharya, "Medical image retrieval with probabilistic multi-class support vector machine classifiers and adaptive similarity fusion," *Computerized Medical Imaging and Graphics*, vol. 32, no. 2, 2008, pp. 95–108.

[56] G. Pavesi and G. Valentini, "Classification of co-expressed genes from DNA regulatory regions," *Information Fusion*, vol. 10, no. 3, 2009, pp. 233–241.

[57] I.W. Selesnick and A.F. Abdelnour, "Symmetric wavelet tight frames with two generators," *Applied and Computational Harmonic Analysis*, vol. 17, no. 2, 2004, pp. 211–225.

[58] I.W. Selesnick and L. Sendur, "Iterated oversampled filter banks and wavelet frames," in Procedding of *SPIE: Wavelet Applications in Signal and Image Processing VIII*, vol. 4119, 2000, pp. 733–744.

[59] I.W. Selesnick, *The Double Density DWT*, in Wavelets in Signal and Image Analysis: From Theory to Practice (Kluwer, 2001).

[60] P. P. Vaidyanathan, *Multirate Systems and Filter Banks* (Prentice Hall, 1993).

[61] N.B. Nill, "A visual model weighted cosine transform for image compression and quality assessment," *IEEE Trans. Comm.*, vol. 33, no. 6, 1985, pp. 551–557.

[62] J.W. Huang, Y.Q. Shi and X.H. Dai, "A segmentation-based image coding algorithm using the features of human vision system," *Journal of Image Graphics*, vol. 4, no. 5, 1999, pp. 400–404.

[63] M. Li, W. Cai and Z. Tan, "A region-based multi-sensor image fusion scheme using pulse-coupled neural network," *Pattern Recognition Letters*, vol. 27, no. 16, 2002, pp. 1948–1956.

[64] S.M. Smith and J.M. Brady, "SUSAN-a new approach to low level image processing," *International Journal Computer Vision*, vol. 23, 1997, pp. 45–78.

INDEX

A

activity level, 20, 139
adverse weather, 18, 19
Alaska, 118
algorithm, vii, ix, 1, 2, 13, 39, 40, 47, 53, 58, 75, 79, 92, 121, 123, 134, 138, 145, 146, 148, 149, 152
amniotic fluid, 57, 61, 65
angiography, 122
assessment, vii, 1, 3, 4, 11, 13, 14, 15, 21, 42, 98, 110, 140, 152
assessment tools, vii, 1

B

bacillus, 57, 58, 61, 63
background information, 31
banks, 123, 128, 152
Beijing, 116, 118
benefits, 38
bioinformatics, 150
biological samples, 57
biomass, 116
biomedical applications, 81
blood flow, 122
bones, 122, 141
brain, 11, 123, 125, 150, 151
brain structure, 150
brain tumor, 125, 150, 151
breast cancer, 125, 150, 151

C

calcification, 125, 149
cancer, 125, 149, 150, 151
challenges, 119
China, 116, 118
classes, 84, 85, 90, 93, 95, 96, 98, 99, 101, 104, 105, 106, 107, 108, 109, 115
classification, viii, 2, 21, 41, 42, 83, 84, 85, 88, 96, 98, 101, 105, 106, 107, 110, 111, 114, 115, 116, 117, 118, 125, 150, 151
cleaning, 114
clinical assessment, 124
clusters(ing), 98, 125
coding, 46, 79, 152
color, viii, 11, 15, 21, 22, 45, 46, 47, 48, 49, 50, 51, 52, 53, 54, 56, 58, 73, 75, 79, 80, 81, 83, 84, 85, 90, 91, 92, 95, 114, 125, 149
complexity, 124
composition, 80
compression, 91, 152
computation, 8, 21, 47, 49, 124, 129
computed tomography, 122, 141
computer, 46, 110, 147
computing, 21, 32, 125, 150
Congress, 116, 119, 147, 149
conservation, 84
contour, 31
correlation, 5, 6, 87, 88, 90, 105, 140
correlation coefficient, 5, 140
cultivation, 84

D

data set, 84, 85, 88, 95, 102, 108, 113, 114, 130, 142, 143
database, 31
decomposition, ix, 8, 10, 11, 12, 20, 80, 121, 129, 132, 136
deep brain stimulation, 151
deforestation, 84, 112, 115
degradation, 84, 88
denoising, 134
depth, 46, 54, 55, 56, 58, 79, 80, 81
Depth-of-Field (DOF), viii, 45, 46, 51, 57, 58, 73
derivatives, 135
detection, 18, 19, 21, 22, 39, 40, 42, 46, 73, 80, 91, 125, 147
detection techniques, 19
deviation, 2, 88, 138
difference threshold, 134, 135
dimensionality, 49, 91
discontinuity, 21
discrimination, 80
diseases, 123
distortions, 3, 6, 11
distribution, 32, 97
DNA, 152

E

ecosystem, 116
electromagnetic, 19
electron, 122
encoding, 91, 134
energy, 3, 6
entropy, 3, 6, 32, 33, 138, 139, 141
environment, 15, 84
ERA, 117
evolution, 149
experimental condition, 79
extraction, viii, 21, 31, 38, 83, 85, 96, 114, 133, 134, 135, 145

F

features extraction, 133
filters, 22, 51, 52, 53, 58, 60, 61, 62, 65, 66, 67, 68, 70, 71, 72, 74, 76, 78, 79, 88, 90, 126, 128, 129, 130
forest fire, 84, 112, 115
forest resources, 115
formula, 58, 98
frost, 88, 89
fused image, vii, viii, ix, 1, 2, 3, 4, 6, 7, 8, 9, 10, 11, 12, 17, 18, 20, 24, 25, 26, 27, 28, 29, 30, 31, 32, 33, 34, 39, 45, 46, 47, 53, 60, 61, 62, 63, 65, 66, 67, 68, 69, 70, 71, 72, 73, 74, 75, 76, 77, 78, 79, 83, 85, 93, 95, 121, 122, 123, 136, 137, 138, 139, 140, 141, 145
fusion, vii, viii, ix, 1, 2, 3, 4, 6, 7, 8, 9, 11, 13, 14, 15, 17, 18, 19, 20, 24, 31, 32, 33, 34, 35, 36, 37, 38, 39, 40, 41, 42, 43, 45, 46, 47, 51, 52, 53, 54, 58, 59, 60, 61, 62, 63, 64, 65, 66, 67, 68, 70, 72, 74, 75, 76, 78, 79, 80, 81, 83, 84, 85, 87, 90, 92, 93, 94, 95, 111, 114, 116, 117, 118, 121, 122, 123, 124, 125, 126, 127, 133, 136, 138, 139, 140, 141, 145, 146, 147, 148, 149, 150, 151, 152

G

gemma, 1
genes, 152
geographical information system (GIS), viii, 83, 84, 85, 110, 111, 112, 113, 114, 115, 117, 118, 119
Georgia, 117
Germany, 119, 148
glucose, 57, 61, 67

H

habitats, 116, 117
hard tissues, 141
haze, 31
histogram, 3, 8, 21, 22, 23, 24, 25, 41, 139
horizontal integration, 112
hue, viii, 83, 91, 93
human body, 122
human brain, 147
human perception, 2, 13

human visual system, vii, 6, 7, 13, 17, 19, 132, 133, 137
hunting, 85
HVS, vii, 17, 19, 21, 24, 137, 145
hybrid, 84

I

illumination, 56, 79
image analysis, 88, 91
image fusion, vii, viii, ix, 1, 2, 4, 6, 7, 8, 11, 13, 14, 15, 18, 19, 24, 38, 39, 40, 41, 42, 43, 45, 46, 47, 52, 59, 60, 62, 63, 64, 66, 68, 70, 72, 74, 76, 78, 79, 80, 83, 84, 85, 90, 92, 114, 116, 117, 118, 121, 122, 123, 124, 125, 126, 127, 133, 136, 140, 145, 146, 148, 149, 151, 152
imagery, 14, 42, 88, 91, 110, 118, 146
imaging modalities, 141
imaging systems, 46
India, 17, 115, 121
integration, 18, 90, 112, 124, 125
intensity-hue-saturation (HIS), viii, 83, 84, 91, 92, 93, 94, 114, 118, 151
iteration, 126

J

Japan, 117

L

lead, 124
learning, 20, 43
legend, 35, 36, 37
lens, 46
light, viii, 18, 19, 45, 58, 80, 91
localization, 135, 145
logging, 84, 115

M

magnetic resonance imaging, 9, 12, 122, 125, 141, 145, 146, 147, 150, 151
Malaysia, 116
management, 112
mapping, 42, 84, 85, 115, 116, 117
marsh, 116
matrix, 88, 91, 98, 101, 105, 108, 110, 128, 129
matrix algebra, 91
measurement, 4, 136, 145
media, 58
median, 133
medical, vii, ix, 1, 18, 46, 79, 121, 122, 123, 124, 125, 126, 136, 137, 141, 145, 146, 147, 148, 149, 150, 151
melting, 112
membership, 125
memory, 124
methodology, 34, 39
microscope, 46, 53, 55, 79, 80
microscopy, viii, 45, 46, 51, 75, 80, 81
military, vii, 1
models, 4, 20, 21, 40, 133, 145, 150, 151
MODIS, 115, 117
modulus, viii, 45, 47, 49, 51, 52, 54, 148
Mongolia, 83, 85, 114, 115, 116, 117, 118, 119
morphology, 125
motivation, 127
multidimensional, 92, 101, 105, 107
multimedia, 81
Myanmar, 115

N

natural resources, 112
Netherlands, 146
neural networks, 20, 85, 118, 125, 126, 149, 150, 152
neurosurgery, 147
nuclear magnetic resonance, 141
nucleus, ix, 121, 123, 134
numerical aperture, 55, 58

O

oil, 116
one dimension, 130
operations, 20, 79, 124
optical microscopy, 46, 47
optical systems, 46
organ, 122
overlap, 91, 96, 101

P

pattern recognition, 98
Philadelphia, 147
plants, 85
polarization, 86, 101
policy, 84
positron emission tomography, 122, 125, 146
preparation, 84
preservation, 4, 33, 117, 140
principal component analysis, viii, 20, 33, 34, 35, 36, 37, 38, 40, 80, 83, 84, 85, 90, 91, 94, 96, 97, 105, 114, 125, 126, 142, 143, 144, 145, 151
principles, vii, 21, 145
prior knowledge, 98
probability, 20, 98, 139
probability density function, 98
project, 132
prototype, 41
purity, 91

R

radar, 84, 86, 88, 90
radiation, 19, 88
radiotherapy, 125, 149
radius, 135
reconstruction, 128, 129, 132
redundancy, 24
refractive index, 58
regression, 150
remote sensing, 81, 84, 116, 118, 119
requirements, 122, 138
resolution, 8, 14, 55, 86, 91, 92, 93, 118, 122, 123, 125
resources, 116, 133
restoration, 79
root, 3, 87
rotations, 124
rules, ix, 121, 123, 145

S

saturation, viii, 83, 91, 93
scaling, 126, 128, 130, 132, 135, 145
sea level, 86
security, 84
selectivity, 126, 145
sensing, 116, 148
sensitivity, 13
sensors, 24, 46
side effects, 124
signals, 5, 88, 128, 147
simple sampling, 145
skewness, 88, 90
smallest univalue segment assimilating nucleus (SUSAN), ix, 121, 123, 125, 127, 129, 131, 133, 134, 135, 136, 137, 139, 141, 143, 145, 147, 149, 151, 152
software, 110
Southeast Asia, 117
Spain, 1, 14
spatial frequency, 138, 139, 141
spatial information, 112
spatial location, 22
specialists, 84
species, 85, 86, 112
spectroscopy, 150
standard deviation, 88, 138, 140, 141
state(s), 2, 112, 122, 146
stratification, 150
stretching, 8
structure, 20, 114, 117, 127, 129, 135
structuring, 124
suppression, 88, 92
surveillance, vii, 1, 17, 18, 31, 39
sustainability, 119
sustainable development, 84
symmetry, 123, 124, 145

T

Taiwan, 115
target, 40, 42
taxonomy, 86, 87, 112, 114
techniques, vii, viii, 17, 18, 19, 20, 21, 23, 31, 33, 34, 35, 36, 37, 38, 39, 46, 75, 80, 81, 83, 84, 85, 88, 90, 92, 93, 95, 96, 113, 114, 117, 118, 119, 122, 124, 126
technology(ies), vii, 111
testing, 34, 75
textural character, 95
texture, 9, 21, 41, 88, 90, 93, 96, 105, 107, 114, 123, 134
time series, 115

tissue, 11, 65, 71, 122
training, 85, 96, 98, 114
transactions, 81
transformation, viii, 83, 85, 87, 90, 91, 93, 94, 96, 114
transmission, 34
treatment, 122, 125, 146, 149
tumor, 122, 125, 150, 151

U

ultrasound, 123, 147
UNESCO, 85, 117
United States (USA), 81, 85, 117, 118, 147

V

variations, viii, 24, 83, 84, 85, 90, 93, 95, 109, 114
vector, 20, 51, 97, 98, 114, 150, 152
vegetation, 116, 117
vision, 13, 18, 39, 41, 46, 152
visual attention, vii, viii, 17, 18, 21, 38, 42
visual images, vii, viii, 17, 18, 19, 20, 21, 24, 25, 31, 38, 39
visual information, viii, 4, 6, 18
visual system, vii, 6, 7, 13, 17, 19, 132, 133, 137, 148
visualization, 13, 125, 131, 134, 146, 149

W

wavelengths, 91
wavelet, viii, 8, 13, 14, 41, 43, 75, 79, 80, 81, 83, 84, 85, 90, 92, 94, 95, 96, 114, 118, 124, 125, 126, 127, 128, 129, 130, 132, 142, 143, 145, 147, 148, 152
West Africa, 117
wild animals, 85
wildlife, 117
windows, 5, 7, 13

Y

yarn, 21, 41